Blacks
in Tennessee
1791–1970

Blacks
in Tennessee
1791-1970

BY LESTER C. LAMON

PUBLISHED IN COOPERATION WITH

The Tennessee Historical Commission

THE UNIVERSITY OF TENNESSEE PRESS

KNOXVILLE

TENNESSEE THREE STAR BOOKS / *Paul H. Bergeron, General Editor*

This series of general-interest books about significant Tennessee topics is sponsored jointly by the Tennessee Historical Commission and the University of Tennessee Press.

Copyright © 1981 by The University of Tennessee Press / Knoxville.
Manufactured in the United States of America.
All Rights Reserved.

Cloth: 1st printing, 1981.
Paper: 1st printing, 1981; 2nd printing, 1993; 3rd printing, 1996.

The paper in this book meets the minimum requirements of the American National Standard for Permanence of Paper for Printed Library Materials.   ∞   The binding materials have been chosen for strength and durability.

       Printed on recycled paper.

Library of Congress Cataloging in Publication Data

Lamon, Lester C., 1942–
        Blacks in Tennessee.
        (Tennessee three star books)
        Bibliography: p.
        Includes index.
        1. Afro-Americans—Tennessee—History. 2. Tennessee—
Race relations. 3. Tennessee—History.
I. Title.   II. Series.
E185.93.T3L36   976.8'00496073   81-3396
ISBN 0-87049-323-X (cloth: alk. paper)   AACR2
ISBN 0-87049-324-8 (pbk.: alk. paper)

Cover Photograph: Detail from "The Fisk Jubilee Singers" (1873), original painting by Edmund Havel and photographic reproduction by Jud Wood, used by permission of Fisk University, Nashville.

ABOUT THE AUTHOR

Lester C. Lamon, who teaches black history at Indiana University at South Bend, is the author of *Black Tennesseans, 1900-1930* (Knoxville: University of Tennessee Press).

To my grandmother, Nelle Lamon

and

My parents, Ruth and Howard Lamon

Preface

Black men and women have played important roles in virtually every significant chapter of Tennessee's history. They have worked, fought, and planned for the state's growth; they have shared in its successes and suffered with its failures. And yet slavery, caste, and segregation also have forced them to live apart and to create for themselves a separate history. To understand the history of black Tennesseans, therefore, one must recognize that they have been both a part of and apart from the developments affecting the dominant white population. Black history was governed by interconnected but separate themes and given meaning by related but separate institutions. An appreciation for the perspective of black Tennesseans provides a necessary and culturally enriching addition to the traditional history of the state.

When the territory later called Tennessee was no more than a trans-mountain wilderness to the west of colonial North Carolina, black slaves accompanied their owners on trading and exploring expeditions. The slaves shared equally in the hardships and occasionally took singular roles in the events preceding statehood. The slave Abraham, for example, was selected for his frontier skills and promised his freedom if he would leave the ill-fated Fort Loudoun in 1760 and travel 300 miles to Charleston, South Carolina, to seek help in breaking an Indian siege. Abraham made the journey safely, delivered his message, and was killed returning to the fort. Later, thousands of black slaves provided much of the labor required to lay a strong agricultural base for the new state. And their presence influenced the formation of particular cultural values and provoked many of the controversies over state rights which drew Tennessee into the Civil War.

As soldiers and laborers, black Tennesseans participated in the defeat of the Confederacy and thus insured their own freedom. Immediately, they took part in and became the focus of much debate as the state adjusted its social, political, and economic institutions to accommodate the changes of war. Then, as second-class citizens in a caste society, they supported schools, opened banks, served in the military, and produced a sizeable portion of Tennessee's wealth during the late nineteenth and early twentieth centuries. Dominated by whites in public affairs, black Tennesseans turned inward, developing their own social institutions and creating a rich, dynamic society that was virtually ignored or seldom taken seriously by whites. As the most vulnerable citizens in the state, however, they suffered severely during the Great Depression, and many left for northern cities during the 1930s and 1940s. But as Tennesseans of long-standing, most blacks remained in their home state.

Encouraged by extensive service in World War II, the expanded function and increased sensitivity of the federal government, and a genuine weariness with racial compromise and waiting, black Tennesseans took to the offense during the 1950s and 1960s. In so doing, they were primarily responsible for transforming the state's society, at last, into one which was formally open and at least constitutionally committed to equality for all its citizens. For one and one-half centuries, black Tennesseans despaired, fought aggressively, showed almost infinite patience, and, above all, simply endured. By the 1950s, however, general attitudes began to change. More and more black Tennesseans declared their determination that, at whatever individual sacrifice, freedom must come, compromise on basic promises of American life must stop, and their dream of equal participation must show tangible signs of becoming a reality.

Tennessee, perhaps more than any other state, does not lend itself to sweeping general statements and evaluations. Geography, economics, race, and political philosophy have divided the state almost from the beginning into three "Grand Divisions." Intrastate competition has reinforced these sectional differences, leaving Tennesseans with many parallel or conflicting traditions rather than merged patterns of outlook and behavior. Differing economic priorities, political loyalties, and racial populations have created superficial dissimilarities in the historical experiences of blacks in the three regions. But running through these experiences, regardless of region, has been a common racial "givenness" — blacks should not expect equality or free association with whites. Everyday manifestations of this racial truth might be more severe in the western regions than in the east, but black Tennesseans always and everywhere encountered what Martin Luther King, Jr., called that "degenerating sense of 'nobodiness.'" Their history is not that of a surrender to this potentially debilitating pressure, but instead is a record of endurance and struggle to throw off the white-imposed stigma of inferiority.

It is not the purpose of the Three Star Books series to offer lengthy monographs with full scholarly apparatus. This book, therefore, aspires to the "big picture," and in many ways it only scratches the surface of its subject. In preparing this volume, I have frequently drawn upon the in-depth research of other historians, but there are gaps in the record that have not been filled adequately, and other areas where existing scholarship is seriously flawed. Examination of the black experience in Tennessee since 1930, for example, has hardly begun. Special notice should be given, however, to the work of Alrutheus Ambush Taylor, black historian and professor of history at Fisk University. His meticulous study of black Tennesseans during the critical years of Reconstruction, published in 1941, is now both a part of their history and a guidepost for those of us who, much later, have come to recognize the important role of blacks in the history of the Volunteer State.

I owe an enormous debt, of course, to those historians and other students of Tennessee's history whose previous works made the preparation of this general survey possible. More specifically, however, Stephen Ash of the University of Tennessee gave valuable assistance in locating many of these sources, and the library staff of Indiana University at South Bend accommodated my countless requests for materials on inter-library loan with a cheerful patience far beyond the normal call of duty. Paul Bergeron combined the skill of the editor with the understanding of a friend, and this book has benefitted enormously from his touch. I also wish to thank Linda Schultz for her aid in typing the manuscript and Al Large of the audio-visual center at Indiana University at South Bend for reproducing several of the photographs. And finally, this project never could have been completed without the support of my wife, Beth, and the enthusiastic encouragement and exhortations of my daughter, Katherine, and my son, Ward.

December 1980   LESTER C. LAMON
South Bend, Indiana

Contents

ILLUSTRATIONS

Blacks
in Tennessee
1791–1970

1. Blacks and Slavery, 1790s to 1860

Louis' mother handed him a small package and, with tears in her eyes, gave her eleven-year-old son a typical motherly admonition: "My son, be a good boy; be polite to every one, and always behave yourself properly." Without his mother's tears Louis Hughes' departure might easily have been mistaken for a visit to grandparents or a neighboring child's birthday party. But Louis' mother was a slave and, therefore, so was he. He was not leaving his home in 1843 for a visit with grandparents or neighbors; instead his owner was taking him to Richmond to be sold in the slave market, and, in fact, he would never see his mother again.

A local man purchased Louis, but a year later, at age twelve, the youngster was back on the slave market. This time he passed quickly through the examination or "show" room, joined the auctioneer on the block, and found himself the property of a second generation Mississippi planter named Edmund McGee. McGee was an early participant in the cotton boom sweeping southwestern Tennessee and northern Mississippi in the mid-1840s and 1850s. Economic and social advancement for the whites required slaves, and in 1844 McGee traveled to Richmond because "Virginia always produces good darkies." Louis, therefore, found himself in the company of sixty other black slaves as he began "a long and wearisome" walk through Tennessee to the Mississippi Delta. Twenty of the slaves were sold along the way before the tired party reached McGee's plantation near Pontotoc on Christmas Eve. After receiving a good scrubbing, Louis found himself in the "great house" being presented as a Christmas gift to Mrs. McGee. For the next twenty years Louis served the McGees.

The city of Memphis flourished as the economic and social axis for western Tennessee, as well as for northern Mississippi. And in 1850 Edmund McGee's social aspirations led him to build a "sumptuous" and "palatial" mansion on the outskirts of the booming river town. At the age of eighteen, Louis was promoted from errand boy to butler. He still remained a slave, however, and he was never allowed to forget that fact. Louis had a privileged position within slavery, but he was not exempt from severe and unpredictable beatings, verbal scorn, and the erratic moods of his mistress. He married a "free Negro" who had been taken from Kentucky and sold to the McGees through the famous Memphis slave yard of Nathan Bedford Forrest, and Hughes fathered three children. But Louis never escaped the trauma of his separation from his mother. He came to identify his routine, his "position," and his environment, but not his person, with his owners. He was "Louis," not "Massa McGee's Louis." And the concept of freedom lived implicitly in the pain and loneliness he experienced when his thoughts, as they so often did, turned to his aborted childhood.

Hughes ran away for the first time in 1852, making it by boat to Indiana before he was captured and returned. Three months later he tried again, and again he failed. Ten years passed and he fled a third time. And a fourth. He failed four times and received severe whippings each time. Finally, in June 1865 he succeeded. He had spent twenty years as a slave in Mississippi and Tennessee, and he had gained freedom by his own initiative. Neither Lincoln's Emancipation Proclamation nor General Lee's surrender had changed Louis' status. In the summer of 1865 Louis Hughes and his wife joined "thousands of others, in search of the freedom of which they had so long dreamed [flocking into Memphis], the city of refuge, some having walked hundreds of miles."

When Louis Hughes entered Tennessee in 1844 as the newly purchased slave of Edmund McGee, he followed a well-beaten path. North Carolina had ceded the area later to be known as "Tennessee" to the federal government, and Congress organized it as the "Territory of the United States South of the River Ohio" in 1790. This new territory beyond the Appalachians was governed under the provisions of the famous Northwest Ordinance of 1787, with one exception—the clause prohibiting slavery. When a census of this territory was completed in 1791, it showed 35,691 people (excluding Indians) living there, 3,417 of whom were black slaves.

Most of these pioneers lived on the ridges and in the valleys of mountainous eastern Tennessee. And for them life was still rather tentative and uncertain. Economic activity (with the exception of land speculation) focused on subsistence and rarely involved long-range capital in-

---

Louis Hughes spent more than thirty years in slavery, mostly in Tennessee. *From* Louis Hughes, Thirty Years A Slave *(1897).*

vestment. Moreover, there was little emphasis upon social advancement and there were few "gentlemen of leisure." In short, conditions on this frontier offered few advantages to owners of large numbers of slaves. Nevertheless, the institution took *legal* root in Tennessee, being transplanted from its practice in North Carolina with little apparent debate. But the new state was also a product of the Revolutionary era—a time when American slavery was at its lowest ebb. Hundreds of black slaves in Virginia and North Carolina had earned their freedom by valorous service to the patriot cause, and, for many Americans, the tyranny of human slavery clashed unfortunately with the revolutionary principles of freedom and equality. Therefore, as the nineteenth century began, neither Tennessee's slave system nor its race relations were very rigid or of great immediate concern.

The black population, however, grew steadily. By 1800, ten thousand new slaves had crossed the mountains from North Carolina or come down the valleys from Virginia with the white families to whom they belonged. In addition, a small but noticeable number of free blacks also resided in the region's scattered communities. These new Tennesseans, free or slave, were almost all native to America and had few self-conscious ties to ancestral Africa. They lived and worked closely with whites, and the regularity of personal contact tended to downplay the importance of enforcing racially restrictive legislation. Tennesseans, for example, inherited rather stringent manumission laws from North Carolina, but Tennesseans also perpetuated a North Carolina practice of freeing slaves in almost commonplace fashion. And while these free blacks did not enjoy all the freedoms of mobility and citizenship of whites, Tennessee's constitution allowed them the important rights of voting and holding property. As long as the numbers were small and existing economic and social roles rather informal, blacks caused little controversy in the state.

Slaves on the early Tennessee frontier rarely lived in large groups, for most slaveholders owned only one or two slaves, or perhaps a slave family. Farms were isolated, and slave and master shared many common experiences. Together they herded cattle and hogs, cleared land, built barns, attended church, and kept an alert eye for hostile Indians. Race provided the necessary distinction between master and slave, thereby making rigidly enforced laws and carefully differentiated tasks of secondary importance. To be sure, whites assigned the duties and roles, but in practice frontier conditions often blurred the distinctions. Slaves in these early years were rarely sold except in settling estates; therefore family relationships and personal attachments had a chance to develop. And, when brought to consider the wisdom and ethics of slavery as an American institution, white Tennesseans often had serious doubts.

Anti-slavery attitudes, in fact, seem to have entered the region with the first permanent settlers. There was little or no sentiment for immediate abolition, but early Tennesseans were men and women firmly grounded in the pioneer spirit of liberty and independence. Slavery contradicted this spirit and its abuses created numerous crises of conscience. Free of the burdens of heavy capital investment and economic dependence upon slave labor, many Tennesseans viewed servitude as temporary (not withstanding its nearly two centuries' presence in the country!). Blacks should be freed when and if deserving, it was argued, and the idea of general emancipation might be fairly entertained when slaves had been adequately prepared by education. The first formal surfacing of these views came in 1797 when Thomas Embree and several other citizens of Washington and Greene counties proposed the formation of an "abolition society" modeled after others founded during the Revolutionary era in Pennsylvania, Delaware, Maryland, and Virginia. Instead of active pursuit of "abolition," however, the main concern of this group focused upon guaranteeing the rights and freedoms of previously emancipated blacks.

Embree and his associates represented an important Quaker faction in early Tennessee, and they were soon joined in their efforts on behalf of slaves and free Negroes by others, particularly the Presbyterian clergy. Thomas Embree's son, Elihu, and Charles Osborn, another Quaker, became increasingly vocal. So did John Rankin, a Presbyterian. Other leading Presbyterian ministers and educators such as Samuel Doak, Gideon Blackburn, and Isaac Anderson argued somewhat less dramatically for greater opportunities for slaves, serious contemplation of emancipation, and the ultimate rejection of the institution on the grounds that it was a curse to God-fearing Christians.

Two anti-slavery nuclei emerged, both in the more heavily populated eastern part of the state. Quaker attitudes predominated in the Greeneville-Jonesboro region and Presbyterian influence centered in Maryville (Blount County). Thomas Embree's earlier "abolition society" apparently never materialized, but between December 1814 and February 1815, Charles Osborn and several other Quakers perfected an organization known as the "Tennessee Society for Promoting the Manumission of Slaves." Branches quickly appeared in most other East Tennessee counties, and in November 1815, members held a state convention at the

Lick Creek Meeting House of Friends in Greene County and adopted the constitution of the "Manumission Society of Tennessee." This organization was to play an important role in the state during the next fifteen years. Its constitution did not call for immediate abolition, but it forbade its members from voting for any public official who opposed the principle of emancipation. Osborn and Rankin urged a much stronger position and, failing in this, moved to Ohio where they took an active part in the national campaign to abolish slavery.

The Manumission Society met little open resistance, but Tennesseans showed no enthusiasm for more radical programs. The Presbyterian clergy and their supporters in Maryville, for example, demonstrated a very moderate approach. They seldom talked of immediate emancipation, but the messages of Blackburn, Anderson, and others contained not only the conviction that slavery ran counter to Christian teachings of love and liberty, but also the warning that if it was not rejected on the principle of love, God would find other means to destroy it. In the short run, individual slaves should be emancipated on the basis of merit, and all slaves should receive better treatment and opportunities for education. In the long run, however, slaveowners must realize that the "peculiar institution" would have to be abandoned. Gideon Blackburn furnished his own example; he owned slaves and he freed several. In 1806 he introduced one of them, John Gloucester, to Union Presbytery as a candidate for licensure. He freed Gloucester, trained him personally, and sponsored his ordination as an evangelist in 1810. Gloucester was sent to Philadelphia where he proceeded to organize the first Presbyterian church for blacks in the United States. At the urging of Isaac Anderson, meanwhile, Union Presbytery bought and freed George Erskine, another locally-owned slave. Anderson had founded the Southern and Western Theological Seminary at Maryville in 1819 and had trained Erskine along with white students at the school. Erskine preached to mixed audiences in East Tennessee throughout the 1820s before being formally ordained and sent to Liberia as a missionary by the General Assembly of the Presbyterian Church in 1829.

The manumission societies in Tennessee received much hopeful attention from the growing anti-slavery forces in the northern states. The publication of two of the nation's earliest anti-slavery newspapers, first by Elihu Embree (Jonesboro, 1819-20) and then by the transplanted New Jersey Quaker, Benjamin Lundy (Greeneville, 1822-24), encouraged this attention. (Embree's paper, first called the *Manumission Intelligencer,* was published weekly, and then as *The Emancipator* appeared monthly. Lundy's *Genius of Universal Emancipation* was published weekly.) Depth of feeling and extent of accomplishment, however, should have tempered the enthusiasm. The "liberal" examples of Gloucester and Erskine were informative—each man left the state. Most opponents of slavery in Tennessee also opposed allowing large numbers of free blacks to remain in the South. Informal race relations could not stand the strain of major adjustment, and advocates of emancipation accepted removal as a necessary corollary to their positions. Nevertheless, anti-slavery forces did play an important role in Tennessee during the early years of the nineteenth century. By use of the courts, regular petitions to the legislature, and the less tangible tool of moral suasion, the forces defended the rights of the free Negro, fought the separation of slave families, and were partly responsible for the banning of the slave trade in Tennessee in 1826. Furthermore, although state law prohibited free blacks from entering the state as new residents, the free Negro population continued to rise at a rate much faster than natural increase could explain—testimony to hundreds of private acts of emancipation. Many former slaves chose or were required to leave the state upon receiving their freedom, but the number of free Negroes in Tennessee rose from 309 in 1800 to 2,727 in 1820 and to 4,555 by 1830.

In these same years of anti-slavery activity, however, Tennessee had sprawled westward, taking its slaves to the tobacco fields and iron furnaces of the central regions and, even more significantly, to the cotton lands of the southwest. Beyond the Cumberland Plateau, the land flattened out and large farms became more efficient. This western expansion, therefore, would have fateful consequences for black Tennesseans. When James Robertson and John Donelson carried the first permanent settlers into the Cumberland Basin during the winter and spring of 1779–80, they took a small number of slaves with them. Two black men, in fact, died on the famous Donelson journey down the Tennessee River from Fort Patrick Henry (present-day Kingsport) and up the Ohio and Cumberland rivers to what would soon become Nashville. The number of settlers grew slowly in the western region, and yet, in the territorial census of 1791, 16.5 percent of that population was already slave, as compared with only 8 percent in the older eastern counties. Here was a glimpse of the future for those who cared to see it. As the Indians were forced to cede more and more of their lands after 1800, migration into and within Tennessee increased enormously, especially in the inviting and sparsely settled areas of the west. As a result, the white population grew by 137 percent between 1800 and 1810, and the slave population by a dramatic 238 percent. Tennessee's center of gravity had shifted west.

As the frontier thus moved westward, it changed character. The newer land suggested exploitation by those with capital to invest in iron furnaces or commercial agriculture. Labor posed a problem for an economy where land was abundant and cheap, and slavery presented a viable, if not philosophically attractive, solution. In the middle part of the state, crops of tobacco and corn were increasingly tended by slaves. And entrepreneurs such as Montgomery Bell and Elias W. Napier used slave labor extensively in developing clusters of iron furnaces in the same region. (In 1820 Montgomery Bell owned more slaves, perhaps, than any other person in Tennessee. At that time he had 83 black slaves.) Cotton was also a product of the area, and it grew in importance after the cotton gin appeared in the state in 1800. By 1804, twenty-four gins operated in Nashville, and in 1820 the state had reached an annual production of 50,000 bales. The critical impact of cotton upon the state's economy and upon the institution of slavery, however, awaited the completion of Tennessee's westward march to the Mississippi River.

In October 1818, Andrew Jackson negotiated the "Chickasaw Purchase," and Tennessee gained access to that portion of the rich Gulf Coastal Plain lying between the Tennessee and Mississippi rivers. This new area came to be designated "West Tennessee," giving the state three geographically distinct regions, each characterized by differing attitudes and dependencies upon slavery. After 1818, settlers moved quickly onto the old Chickasaw land, and they took the trappings of cotton production with them. By 1830, Tennessee's cotton output had jumped sharply and of the 140,000 new residents in West Tennessee, 26,161 or just under 20 percent were slaves (see Appendix). Continued economic development of the west depended heavily upon cotton, and cotton (as well as other large-scale agriculture) had become increasingly dependent upon slave labor. The purchase price of slaves underscored this connection; simple laws of supply and demand were primarily responsible for price increases of as much as $300 or $400 per slave between 1820 and 1835.

Economic considerations now made the task of slavery's opponents progressively more difficult. Pocketbook issues interfered with appeals to conscience and fairness. Up to this point, limits on the success of emancipation forces in Tennessee had been mostly a matter of race rela-

---

When Territorial Governor William Blount ordered a census taken in the "Southwest Territory" in 1791, approximately 10 percent of the population was black. *From the First Census of the United States.*

[56]

Schedule of the whole number of persons in the territory of the United States of America, South of the River Ohio, as taken on the last Saturday of July 1791, by the Captains of the Militia within the limits of their respective districts.

	Free white males of 21 years and upwards; including heads of families.	Free white males under 21 years.	Free white females including heads of families.	All other persons.	Slaves.	Total of each county.	Total of each district.
WASHINGTON DISTRICT.							
Washington	1009	1792	2524	12	535	5872	
Sullivan	806	1242	1995	107	297	4447	
Greene	1293	2374	3580	40	454	7741	
Hawkins	1204	1970	2921	68	807	6970	
South of Fr. Broad	681	1082	1627	66	163	3619	
							28649
MERO DISTRICT.							
Davidson	639	855	1288	18	659	3459	
Sumner	404	582	854	8	348	2196	
Tennessee	235	380	576	42	154	1387	
							7042
	6271	10277	15365	361	3417		35691

Note. There are several Captains who have not as yet returned the Schedules of the numbers of their districts, namely: In Greene County, three—in Davidson, one—and South of French-Broad, one district.

September 19th, 1791.

Wm: **BLOUNT.**

tions. Slavery constituted an unfortunate presence, but tens of thousands of free Negroes would be unbearably disruptive to white tradition and social preference. As the economies of Middle and West Tennessee developed, however, and as social hierarchies based upon wealth and leisure evolved, advantage began to replace expediency as a reason for rejecting emancipation. Complicating the task of the emancipationists was the increasing presence of the American Colonization Society in Tennessee. The limited goals and even more limited actions of this organization seemed to offer an ideal solution to whites who could not shake their doubts about slavery — endorsement of its program of removing blacks to Liberia provided a salve for the conscience without seriously threatening the institution. Furthermore, the rubric of colonization also reinforced a staunch and growing proslave argument for removal of free Negroes from the state.

On the surface, support for colonization seemed to reveal a serious and growing anti-slavery sentiment in Tennessee. Andrew Jackson served as a vice-president of the national organization (1819–22), the legislature formally endorsed the group in 1827, and in 1829 the Tennessee Colonization Society, led by the prominent Nashville educator Dr. Philip Lindsley, received a state charter. Tennessee became an active field for national agents such as James Birney, who concluded optimistically in 1833 that "all that is wanting . . . to disburden [Tennesseans] of slavery in a reasonable time is to defray the cost of a comfortable conveyance to a safe and pleasant home." Without a strong conviction that slavery was a moral evil, however, the burden of expense proved almost insurmountable. It cost approximately $180 for the American Colonization Society to resettle a freed slave in Liberia — and this did not guarantee either a "comfortable conveyance" or a "safe and pleasant home." Several Middle Tennessee planters (such as James K. Polk's kinsman, Andrew J. Polk) and the Presbyterians of East Tennessee made regular contributions, and in 1833, the legislature appropriated ten dollars to the Society for each black person removed from Tennessee to Liberia (not to exceed a total of $500 per year). But this support did not go far, and the Tennessee Colonization Society brought no realistic change in either the institutional foundation of slavery in the state or the prospects and opportunities for blacks held in bondage.

The number of blacks sent from Tennessee to Liberia (or Haiti, in a few cases) cannot accurately be determined, but it was not large. At most, it could not have been much more than two thousand. For many of those slaves freed on the condition that they emigrate, the prospects of freedom were exhilarating. Such was the case for ninety slaves freed by Montgomery Bell in 1853. They were transported to Savannah, Georgia, at his expense, and from there they sailed for Liberia on December 16. The parting words of one older emigrant were: "we will never stop thanking to the Lord for his [Bell's] goodness to us." The fate of these colonists is not known, but for most of those who returned to the "homeland" that they had never before known, life was not easy. The land was not as fertile, the climate was more hostile, and the diseases were new. The missionary George Erskine, for example, died within a year of reaching Liberia. Colonization, therefore, provided no viable remedy for the evils of slavery. In fact, by 1830 the idea was siphoning off some of the strength of more vigorous emancipation stances and, in time, became associated with solving the problem of the continuing presence of free Negroes rather than being a scheme for eliminating slavery.

Sensing the hardening of pro-slavery views and a wavering of anti-slavery sentiment, emancipation proponents gathered strength for a major (and ultimately final) thrust at their foe. Opportunity dictated the timing of these efforts. In May 1834, sixty delegates met in Nashville to revise or rewrite the original statehood constitution of 1796. Voters had approved the call for this convention out of a desire to remove special tax privileges enjoyed by the "lords of the soil" and to reorganize representative government along more democratic lines. When the delegates convened, however, they found themselves confronted with thirty petitions asking that the new constitution contain some provision for either the immediate or gradual abolition of slavery in Tennessee. The anti-slavery petitioners came mostly from East Tennessee, a region where the size of the slave population had remained relatively stable in the previous two decades. Forty-two of the sixty delegates at the convention, however, came from Middle and West Tennessee—regions whose slave populations had grown dramatically since 1810. By raising the question of the future of slavery in the state, anti-slavery forces in the east created the most thorny and controversial issue of the convention. The decisions reached by this special assembly did not come easy, but when made, they would serve as a reliable indicator as to the future prospects for blacks in Tennessee.

Fearing that open debate on the slavery issue might consume a great amount of time and deflect the body from its goals of tax reform and political reorganization, convention leaders referred the anti-slavery petitions to a special Committee of Propositions and Grievances. After consideration and then reconsideration this committee reported its recommendation that the "perplexing question" of emancipation be shelved. Speaking for the committee, John A. McKinney of Hawkins County admitted that slavery was an evil, but he argued the "utter impracticability" of the abolition proposals contained in the existing petitions. Furthermore, McKinney suggested an end to consideration of the question because the "wisest heads and the most benevolent hearts [have] not been able to answer [it] in a satisfactory manner." Fear of slave insurrections such as the recent Nat Turner rebellion in Virginia did not play a major part in the convention's open deliberations, but McKinney indicated that this concern did lurk beneath the surface. His report postulated that newly freed slaves would be "strongly tempted" to join their remaining "brothers in chains" in a "concert" to "exterminate the white race and take "possession of the country." The strongest key to the committee's rejection of the petitions remained, however, the threat they offered to traditional race relations in the state.

In 1834, most Tennesseans probably still agreed publicly with John McKinney; slavery was undesirable. But they, likewise, had no desire to adjust social, political, or economic relations in such a way as to imply or encourage greater racial equality. Many still held out hope that slavery should not "be perpetual" in the state, but their will to work toward such a demise was weak. It was more politic and less frustrating to join McKinney in his endorsement of the private colonization societies. Be patient, he told the anti-slavery petitioners, "Providence has already opened [this] door of hope, which is every day opening wider and wider." Whether this statement was a tactic of political conciliation at the convention or a genuine exercise in wishful thinking is unimportant; a stronger stand against slavery could not be attained. In fact, the forcing of the issue actually caused the constitutional architects of 1834 to feel a greater necessity to make explicit the legal foundations of the "peculiar institution" than had been the case with their forebears in 1796. The delegates not only rejected the petitions for gradual abolition, they also, by a vote of 30 to 27, included a provision in the new constitution denying a future legislature the right to pass any law allowing "the emancipation of slaves without the consent of their owner or owners."

The debate over emancipation, likewise, hardened attitudes toward free Negroes. Discussions of slavery and race relations almost inevitably turned attention to the anomalous position of free blacks. Delegates at the convention voted 33 to 23 to reduce this inconsistency by denying free Negroes the franchise in the new constitution. In one sense, this action was paradoxical—a major purpose of the convention had been to increase democracy and voting rights. But in another sense, it was also a self-fulfilling prophecy. John McKinney argued against emancipation on the grounds that free blacks experienced a condition which was "the most forlorn and wretched that can be imagined." Removal of the franchise certainly encouraged a verification of this assessment.

Slavery in Tennessee had weathered its last significant internal challenge. Continued growth of the plantation system in West Tennessee and resentment against the increasingly vocal abolition forces in the North hardened and widened pro-slavery support in the state. In addition, new restrictions began to erode the rights of free Negroes "like a torrent of rain on a grassless slope." As one participant in the 1834 convention had remarked, when the new constitution referred to "we the people", it meant "we the *free white* people . . . and the free white people only."

By the 1830s and 1840s recognizable patterns had emerged in the lives of the growing black population in Tennessee. If Louis Hughes had observed carefully as he trudged through Tennessee in 1844, he would have seen variations in these patterns from east to west, but they would have been differences of degree and not substance. Slaves lived in smaller groups in the east and their proportion of the total population was higher in the west; the free Negro community was proportionately larger in the east; and the slave trade was more active in the west. As individuals, families, and communities, however, most black Tennesseans (free or slave) shared common work experiences, fears, values, and social opportunities. And, their expectations for the future were not bright.

In East Tennessee, blacks continued to live in small groupings, much as they had in the early frontier days of the late eighteenth century. Only where the valleys flattened out and where transportation gave easier access to commercial markets did any semblance of the "plantation life" occur. By 1840, slaves and free blacks still made up only 9.4 percent of the population in this region, hardly changed from 8.5 percent in 1800. For blacks in Middle Tennessee, however, the chances of living in a significant racial community improved. Average slaveholdings remained small (less than five slaves per owner), but in tobacco growing areas such as Montgomery County, cotton districts like Maury County, and the iron producing region of Dickson County, the average increased to perhaps twelve slaves per owner. Furthermore, Middle Tennessee produced some of the largest slave concentrations in the state—Montgomery Bell, for example, owned 332 slaves in 1850, and, in the entire region at that date, 422 slaveowners held at least 20 slaves. In 1840, slaves and free blacks made up 26.5 percent of the total population of Middle Tennessee. Higher racial percentages and larger average holdings developed in West Tennessee, improving opportunities for intra-group contact among slaves. Cotton was the dominant crop, and in southwestern counties such as Fayette and Haywood, black slaves outnumbered whites. In 1840, the black population of West Tennessee exceeded 30 percent of the region's total and was increasing steadily (see Appendix).

The regional distribution of Tennessee's small free Negro population was in inverse proportion to the relative size of the slave contingent — highest in East Tennessee and lowest in West Tennessee. In the east many free blacks lived in the countryside, in drafty shacks on the most hilly and marginal land. Here, as throughout the state, they occupied the anomalous status of being technically free, but limited by local racial custom in their right to mingle casually with white freemen. Such an existence could mean great isolation and loneliness, but as the historian Ira Berlin has pointed out, it could also provide "a degree of autonomy and a chance to escape the pressures of a white-dominated world." Approximately one-third of the state's free Negroes resided in towns, especially if they remained in Middle or West Tennessee. Here they either lived in close proximity to their white employers or occupied "quarters" on the outskirts or in undesirable locations (swampy land, near railroad tracks, for example) of the city. Under such circumstances, the practical distinction between slave and freeman was negligible. Free blacks, even before the 1834 Constitutional Convention, enjoyed a steadily narrowing concept of freedom. They had already lost the right to testify against whites in court and also were required to register with the county clerk and carry their registration certificate when leaving their home county.

While few black Tennesseans were natives of Africa, many did come from outside the state. The interstate slave trade may have slackened after its prohibition in 1826, but it certainly never halted. West Tennessee contained virtually no slaves in 1820 and over 56,000 by 1840. These could not have been simply transfers from the other two regions, because East Tennessee's slave population was very small and the number of slaves in Middle Tennessee was also increasing dramatically. Overall, the state's slave population expanded by more than 300 percent between 1810 and 1840. One of the most important slavetrading partnerships in the South was that of two Tennessee residents, Isaac Franklin and John Armfield. Estimates indicate that this firm sold an average of 1,200 slaves per year during the expansionary period, 1828–35. Not all of these sales took place in Tennessee, but many did. Economic law superseded civil law, and the slave trade brought thousands of new blacks to the state. And, in spite of the claims of southern slaveowners and their later apologists, the slave trade meant the regular disruption of slave families and other black social institutions.

Most black Tennesseans had a tearful mother, child, or other loved one in their backgrounds, and the fear of being sold remained a constant psychological burden in their lives. This fear might easily have retarded the formation of strong family bonds among slaves, but, as historian Herbert Gutman has shown, this was not normally the case. In fact, the high incidence of sales actually may have strengthened black family attachments. Louis Hughes never lost the keen memory of his mother, and after finally escaping successfully, he risked recapture by returning to rescue his wife. Accurate estimates of how often slave families in Tennessee were actually disrupted by sale are hard to obtain.

The state was not a "breeding" area where slaves were produced primarily for sale to other states, for its own demand had not been completely satisfied when the Civil War broke out. But this did not mean that slaves born or brought into the state had no reason to fear being sold. One slave, for example, later recalled having been sold four times without leaving Franklin County. More informative, however, is the fact that over 26,000 slaves were sold outside the state between 1850 and 1860. It has been estimated that these sales resulted in the actual disruption of between 13 and 27 percent of all slave families in Tennessee. Black fears for the preservation of the family, therefore, were firmly grounded in experience. The hold on family ties was fragile, but it was no less precious. Ancestral naming patterns and oral traditions became protective devices, and if these failed, there was reunion in the after life. As a slave in Shelbyville wrote to his wife back in Virginia in 1833, "I hope with gods helpe that I may be abble to rejous with you on the earth [but] . . . in glory there weel meet to part no more forever."

Slaves in Tennessee enjoyed few social opportunities and had to rely heavily upon the family. Most lived in small groups, had very limited mobility, and found it difficult to escape the increasingly fearful and watchful eyes of their white masters. Church services offered some relief to social isolation. Whites often restricted and meddled in black religious activities, but they rarely prohibited them. On the big plantations, traveling preachers, black and white, conducted services with the master's approval. In the smaller communities of Middle and East Tennessee, slaves and free Negroes regularly attended church with whites. They had to sit in the back rows or in a special balcony, but they were usually considered formal members of the congregation. All denominations gave effort to their "Negro missions," but none as successfully as the Methodists and Baptists. Like most lower and middle class whites, blacks preferred the evangelical style. When given the opportunity to have their own churches, as they most often did in the cities, slaves and free Negroes alike treasured the opportunity on Sunday to release feelings and enthusiasm which had been consciously suppressed in their daily routines. Baptist and Methodist services encouraged this personal participation. But even in their own churches, the style was more "liberating" than the theological substance.

There were many black preachers, but perhaps the most prominent black religious figure in Tennessee before the Civil War was the Reverend Nelson Merry. Merry succeeded a white pastor at Nashville's black First Baptist Church in the 1840s, and he continued his Nashville ministry until 1884. He depended upon white help to build and maintain his church and at his death was praised by the white community for his "character, wisdom, and prudence." Merry could not have enjoyed such support and tenure had he not accommodated generally with white demands, and yet, black membership in his church soared at one point to 2,800. Real freedom may have awaited the "coming of glory," but it could at least be tasted for a few hours on Sunday.

In addition to the family and the church, a black sense of community also cushioned the potentially debilitating weight of slavery and oppression. Free blacks often by virtue of family ties, interacted regularly with slaves as a part of this community—race, not legal status, being the major determinant of social bonds. In Tennessee, the strength of the black community depended upon the size of the black population and the attitudes of controlling whites. But even on the most repressive cotton plantations in West Tennessee, slave quarters regularly served as gathering places for storytelling and as a "clearinghouse of news concerning family members . . . births, deaths, illnesses and separations." As historian Gladys Fry has pointed out, however, relationships in the black community also performed the special function of helping to "preserve the slave's or free Negro's sense of self-identity, of knowing who he was and how he perceived his world." Given the lack of control a slave or even a free Negro had over such basic individual decisions as where and for whom one worked, what one ate, and how one's body was treated, the supporting role of black social institutions could not be minimized.

Black slaves and freemen played an increasingly essential role in Tennessee's rapidly growing economy. This economy remained heavily agricultural, and most blacks, free or slave, on small farms or large plantations, shared a common work experience. They chopped cotton, cared for tobacco, worked corn and wheat fields, or tended livestock. Some performed skilled tasks as blacksmiths or carpenters, but even here they usually worked in support of agriculture. The two major exceptions came in the iron foundries of Middle Tennessee and in the work of house servants throughout the state. Several thousand slaves, for example, served as miners, colliers, and moulders at iron furnaces concentrated within a reasonable transportation distance of the Cumberland and Tennessee rivers. But if not employed in agricultural jobs, black slaves most likely shared Louis Hughes' experience as a domestic servant. There, they might enjoy, like Hughes, the benefits of superior clothing and somewhat less physically strenuous tasks, but they did not escape mental anguish, poor diet, and harsh physical beatings. These abuses were common to Tennessee's slaves, regardless of economic function. Meat (bacon), meal, and molasses comprised a monotonous slave fare. Beatings, however, were less predictable and the most dehumanizing feature of a slave's life. Louis Hughes dreaded them, and he was frustrated by the caprice with which his mistress used the whip. Hughes burned with indignation, recalling on one occasion that "after the first burst of tears, the feeling came over me that I was a man, and it was an outrage to treat me so—to keep me under the lash day after day."

Hardships, frustration, and abuse did not prevent blacks from thriving in Tennessee, producing considerable wealth for whites and increasing in numbers. Yet, unless shielded by unusually close personal attachments with influential whites, all blacks in the state faced tightening restrictions in the 1840s and 1850s. These limitations, imposed by a more fearful and less relaxed master class, severely reduced black chances for eventual freedom. For those 5,524 free Negroes in Tennessee in 1840 or for those few who gained freedom after that date and, in defiance of law remained in the state, what advantages could they expect? Most importantly, they survived in spite of the widely touted belief that blacks could not manage on their own in a competitive situation. Poverty encouraged a higher mortality rate than for whites, but free Negroes enjoyed the undeniable, if intangible, asset of freedom. Freedom opened a "crack" in the door of the future. They had the opportunity to accumulate property, enjoyed somewhat greater mobility than slaves, and were in a better position to earn money—frequently for use in purchasing the freedom of other members of their family. Some free blacks obtained considerable skills, especially as barbers, bricklayers and draymen, but even among these "privileged" freemen, economic security remained vulner-

able to the priorities of a caste system. In practice, the advantages of
free Negroes in antebellum Tennessee were marginal and insecure. In a
society based upon race instead of class, the future of free Negroes was
closely tied with the future of slavery in the state. As a white slaveowner
abruptly observed, "you may manumit a slave but you cannot make him
into a white man." And a free Negro who measured his liberty against
that of whites in Tennessee clearly found it wanting.

During the ten years leading up to the Civil War, new restrictions and
heightened fears placed additional curbs on black opportunities. The
rising volume of abolitionist rhetoric outside the South stirred long-
standing fears of slave revolt and fanned the flames of sectional resentment. White Tennesseans felt these pressures, and they were determined
to minimize interference in what otherwise was a decade of expansion,
prosperity, and optimism. More land came under cultivation, cotton
prices rose, and slave labor became more profitable. Internal security
received new and sometimes irrational attention. Blacks, regardless of
legal status, were vulnerable to whatever expressions white values and
fears might take.

As the most blatant contradiction to white racial ideals and expectations, free blacks drew new attention. It became necessary to define
exactly what made a person a "Negro," and the Tennessee legislature declared that anyone with one black ancestor in the three previous generations should be subject to existing racial restrictions. Almost all civil
rights had been removed prior to and including the Constitutional Convention of 1834. Mobility was severely curtailed, and the exercise of
"freedom" by 1850 meant little more than the right to hold real property
and maintain residence in the state. As one legislator explained, however, new restrictions on free Negroes would never satisfy some white
Tennesseans. "Their mere presence," he said, "the simple act of walking
our streets, and travelling our highways by the farms of the countryside
is sufficient to incite insurrection in the slaves." The hysteria generated
by John Brown's raid on Harper's Ferry, Virginia, in 1859 actually caused
the Tennessee legislature to consider seriously a bill requiring free blacks
either to leave the state or face re-enslavement.

The Civil War intervened before expulsion occurred, but not before
new steps were taken to limit the growth of the free Negro population.
On the one hand, in a display of great arrogance in 1858, Tennessee
"made it lawful" for a freeman to "choose" to become a slave! There is
no evidence that any blacks took advantage of this golden opportunity,
although many free persons found themselves illegally *forced* into bond-

age. On the other hand, however, whites did take steps to stop the emancipation process completely and to force anti-slavery dissenters into flight or silence. With few exceptions, anti-slavery sentiment in Tennessee had already been reduced to the lowest common denominator of colonization. And, in effect, colonization had become more of a scheme to hold down the numbers of free Negroes than a program to phase out slavery. In 1853, the legislature gave further support to this plan by requiring that emancipation be accompanied by removal to Liberia.

Previous suppression of anti-slavery activities had involved more than defeat at the 1834 convention. The case of Amos Dresser bears witness. Dresser, a Bible salesman from Ohio and a member of the American Anti-Slavery Society, was found in Nashville in 1835 with several anti-slavery tracts. He was brought before a vigilance committee and sentenced to receive twenty lashes from a police officer on the public square. Dresser took his punishment and left town. But in 1836 the distribution of such abolitionist literature and the giving of abilitionist speeches "fell under the legislative hammer," and formal penalties now involved prison sentences of between five and twenty years. Enforcement of these laws restricting emancipation and penalizing anti-slavery agitation varied throughout the state. Activity, for example, did not altogether cease in the Maryville area, and large and influential slaveowners such as Elias Napier and Montgomery Bell in Middle Tennessee could ignore emancipation laws without feeling threatened. Nevertheless, the restrictions had their effect; the free black population virtually stabilized while white and slave numbers continued to grow.

Slave activities also drew considerable attention in the decade before the Civil War. At the heart of much of Tennessee's new agricultural prosperity and the historical foundation upon which its bi-racial society was organized, slavery demanded protection. White Tennesseans answered rising abolitionist agitation in the North with new restrictions on slaves, re-opening of the slave trade, and frequent paranoia over the possibility of slave revolt. Chinks in the slave system were "caulked" and blacks suffered.

Tennessee's slave "code" involved several layers of legislative statutes, city ordinances, judicial interpretations, and informal practices. Technically, a slave in antebellum Tennessee enjoyed the protection of legal counsel, grand jury indictment, and trial by jury, but such "paper" protection is of limited value when it, alone, supports a dependent class. Black slaves depended upon whites to protect their rights—the same whites who enslaved them in the first place, insisted upon their social inferiority, and regularly violated their sense of human dignity. Slaves were extremely vulnerable, and whites were inconsistent in applying both the protections and restrictions of the law to blacks. Blacks generally existed for white convenience, and during the 1850s this condition produced greater attention to restriction than protection.

Fear that slaves might come in contact with lurking abolitionists, be led to run away by radical propaganda, or incited to revolt or other crime while under the influence of alcohol caused whites to impose numerous new constraints. Legislation in Memphis, for example, prohibited all preaching by blacks and limited any type of teaching to that having the specific permission of the mayor and carried out under police supervision. Laws throughout the state practically removed the slave's right to hire out his or her own labor and required written permission from one's owner before engaging in any trade, commerce, or other economic endeavor. Whites who allowed or participated in such forbidden activities also faced new penalties. Although often ignored, these restrictions could be quickly and easily enforced should the desire to limit slave (or free Negro, for that matter) mobility arise. Curfews in Memphis, Nashville, and other towns supplemented the long-standing premise that a slave had no legal privileges off his or her master's property without a pass. In 1856, the legislature encouraged these limits with a greatly expanded system of civilian patrolling. Even traditional Tennessee historians have admitted that during the 1850s "in nearly every instance, punishments were increased and privileges and immunities were lessened and circumvented."

No action by white Tennesseans, however, indicated as forcefully their commitment to slavery as did the reopening of the interstate slave trade. In 1855 the Tennessee General Assembly repealed its 1826 prohibition, and this ended the state's "exceptionally long" period of legal self-deception. Perhaps the repeal was an act of exasperation at non-enforceability, but more likely, given the meager efforts made at enforcement, it was a positive act of commitment to the institution of slavery. Debate had ended.

The prohibition in 1826 had been more anti-slave trader than anti-slavery. Slave traders had frequently exploited the great demand for slaves that accompanied western expansion by selling stolen, defective, or undesirable (criminal) "merchandise." They developed a reputation as an unsavory group of shysters who could not be trusted and whose profession was not socially acceptable. But there was nothing wrong with buying slaves, only dealing in them. The 1826 statute did not prohibit slaveowners or prospective slaveowners from going to the slave market in Richmond (as Edmund McGee had done when he purchased Louis Hughes) to buy slaves and import them to Tennessee. Furthermore, the law was also relaxed enough to allow slave traders to lead their unfortunate "gangs" through the state on the way to Mississippi, New Orleans, or elsewhere. Sales were, of course, technically forbidden. But loosely enforced statutes did not stand in the way of enterprising individuals who sought to use Tennessee's central location in the South to participate actively and profitably in the interstate slave trade. Nashville had become a significant slave-trading center prior to 1855, and Memphis had developed into one of the most important markets in the entire South.

By the time that formal prohibition ended, a dynamic and ambitious young slave-trader named Nathan Bedford Forrest had already established himself as a major figure in Memphis. He operated openly and with impunity while importing slaves from Virginia, Georgia, South Carolina, and Kentucky for re-sale in West Tennessee, Mississippi, and Texas. Forrest had a reputation, even among slaves, for running one of the most comfortable and efficient slave-pens in the South. A former slave reminisced about being sold there as a child: "I was young but I remember well some things I saw there. The yard[,] a kind of square stockade of high boards with two room negro houses around, say three sides of it and high board fence too high to be scaled[,] on the other side . . . We were all kept in these rooms but when an auction was held or buyers came we were brought out and paraded two or three times around a circular brick walk in the center of the stockade[.] The buyers would stand near by and inspect us as we went by, stop us and examine us. Our teeth, & limbs and a Doctor generally if there were sick negroes." Forrest's reputation for reliability and well-cared-for slaves did not prevent him, however, from knowingly buying and selling free Negroes on occasion. Louis Hughes' wife, Matilda, passed through Forrest's market twice, although he knew from the start that she "was only sold to prevent her from getting her freedom." Forrest sold at least 1,000 slaves per year during the late 1850s, and his annual earnings averaged near $100,000.

Slavery certainly had its rewards for many white Tennesseans, but the rewards did not come without some uneasiness. Since Virginia's Nat Turner rebellion in 1831, southerners had been wary of slave unrest. Vocal and insistent abolitionism fueled their fears, and the rise of the Republican party in the mid-1850s produced virtual paranoia at election time. In 1856 Tennessee was rife with rumors of slave insurrection. Large sections of Middle and West Tennessee bordered on panic. A young slave girl had suggested that a revolt among West Tennessee slaves was planned to coincide with the fall election, and whites reacted swiftly to contain the "uprising." Patrols were strengthened in Nashville and Memphis, and numerous slaves were arrested in Fayette and Tipton counties. Two weeks after the news of the "plots" in West Tennessee began to circulate, panic of major dimensions broke out in the iron district of northern Middle Tennessee. Several slaves were executed and others beaten severely for allegedly taking part in a plan to capture Clarksville and to bring upheaval in several counties on both sides of the state boundary with Kentucky. Reports of powder kegs and mass attacks, however, proved groundless.

The fear of slave revolt in Tennessee was no less real for a lack of solid evidence to confirm the threat. Thorough investigation turned up nothing more concrete than "loose talk" in the slave quarters. But the racial atmosphere in the South was becoming overheated and occasionally produced brutal suppression of black revolts which, in the view of historian Charles Dew, "existed only in the panic-stricken minds of white southerners." New fears of a slave insurrection were aroused in the Volunteer State in 1858, and each new threat brought more restrictions and harsher treatment for black Tennesseans.

Fear of bodily harm and concern for the maintenance of white supremacy supported sound economic reasons for protecting slavery in Tennessee. High prices for staple goods such as cotton and tobacco led to a 30 percent increase in the amount of improved land in the state during the 1850s. Increased acreage required more labor, and this meant slaves. Laws of supply and demand bid up the average value of slaves in Tennessee from $547 in 1850 to $888 in 1860, and, on the eve of the Civil War, slaves represented 34 percent of the taxable property in the state. Some free blacks in cities like Memphis and Nashville shared in this prosperity by accumulating significant wealth of their own, but most black Tennesseans in 1860, as in 1796, were propertyless slaves. As slaves, their economic importance had grown, and correspondingly, their opportunities for freedom diminished.

By 1860 slavery had become an important social and economic institution in Tennessee—a status it had not held in 1791. Settlement had begun in the mountainous eastern part of the state, and in 1860, conditions and attitudes in this region still did not encourage the use of slave labor. During the first half of the nineteenth century, however, the center of population shifted westward where geographic conditions supported larger farm units. As thousands of slaves fulfilled the growing demand for labor, the casual and essentially negative attitude of early Tennessee settlers was replaced with a growing commitment to slavery as a positive force. Whites defended slavery not only for its economic importance, but also for the control it offered to race relations. By 1860, the 283,019 blacks made up 25 percent of the overall population and formed a majority in three counties. Few whites considered blacks their equal, and slavery became a comfortable verification of these beliefs. Consequently, anti-slavery sentiment received less and less support, and the anomalous caste of free Negroes faced more comprehensive restrictions. As abolitionist attacks from outside the South became more threatening, whites built new and higher walls around their "peculiar institution." Even East Tennessee, which never became rabidly pro-slave or achieved a strong southern self-identity, turned decidedly anti-abolitionist. Blacks living in Tennessee, therefore, had little cause for optimism. Personal relations between the races had become formal, constrained, and fearful. Louis Hughes sensed the negative flow in race relations and alternated between despondency and indignation. Never, however, did he relinquish the will to influence his future. Other black Tennesseans demonstrated similar resiliency.

2. Unfulfilled Promises, 1860 to 1880s

When Louis Hughes and his wife arrived in Memphis on July 4, 1865, they encountered throngs of black refugees celebrating a most meaningful Independence Day. Among the numerous orators addressing the noisy, milling crowds, a tall, light-skinned black man with "Indian" features undoubtedly demanded attention. Edward Shaw was "an able, forcible . . . earnest, and . . . eloquent speaker" who could capture and hold an audience, even on a hot steamy July day. If Hughes and his wife passed Shaw, they most certainly would have paused to listen. Shaw held strong opinions on human rights and equality, and he expressed them vigorously and regularly during the crucial, early years following emancipation.

Ed Shaw was born in Kentucky during the 1820s, grew up in Indiana, and moved to Tennessee as a free Negro in 1852. Why Shaw came to Tennessee is not clear—since free Negroes had been forbidden by the legislature in 1831 to enter the state—but he settled in Memphis and apparently steered clear of racial controversy. He was, however, an ambitious and sensitive man, and he recognized new possibilities for racial and personal advancement generated by the Civil War. Shaw avoided a Confederate draft of free Negroes and considered enlisting in the Union army, but he resented its policies of using blacks principally as laborers and denying them promotion to commissioned officer status. He eventually chose not to take an active role in what he interpreted as a "white man's fight." And Shaw refused to praise Lincoln for emancipation, calling the famous proclamation merely "a war measure, [just] an incident of the war."

Instead of subjecting himself directly to unsympathetic white military authorities, Edward Shaw chose to stay in Memphis and open a saloon and gambling house. His patrons were the thousands of blacks who, like Louis Hughes, sought out the city as a refuge and a place of opportunity. Shaw's ambition, oratorical abilities, and aggressive personality marked him as a leader within this dynamic black community, and he both attracted and demanded attention. He entered politics on the side of the "Radical" Republicans and soon became a major political force in Memphis. Shaw's subsequent twenty-year career as a public figure was marked by a controversial mixture of commitment to meaningful freedom for black Tennesseans and a desire for personal advancement.

Ed Shaw expected that his influence among the new black voters should bring him proper rewards, and he did not hesitate to make his grievances public—even when they indicted other Radical Republicans. His complaints, however, stemmed not so much from personal slights as they attacked white political authorities who refused to grant significant and unprejudiced recognition to *all* blacks. The majority of Republican voters in Memphis and a high percentage statewide were black, and Shaw argued loudly and often bitterly that they should be allowed to hold office and participate in policy-making. Shaw occasionally split with the party, dealing with the Democrats or running for office independently. In 1870, for example, he accused the regular Republican hierarchy of blatant racism and placed his own name on the ballot for a seat in Congress. Shaw had no chance of winning the election, having split the party's vote, but in thus becoming Tennessee's first black candidate for Congress, he intended to teach white politicians "that we are not to be led by the nose."

Edward Shaw experienced more political failures than successes, but he was never "led by the nose." For twenty years he fought for his own and his race's civil rights. He served short terms as wharfmaster, coal oil inspector, and Shelby County commissioner, but he could not consistently overcome the combined effect of white power and pervasive white racism. He was flexible in his political alliances but not in his principles. He refused to compromise on the sensitive issue of mixed schools and campaigned openly for the passage of a federal civil rights bill and the partial repudiation of the state debt.

Politics dominated Shaw's career, but in the mid-1880s he left the arena in frustration. His uncompromising principles and unpredictable party loyalties had drawn much abuse, and he now chose the less controversial life of an active Mason and prominent member of the African Methodist Episcopal Church. He had managed to gain entry to the Memphis bar during his period of political activism, and the last years before his death in 1891 were spent in this profession. Edward Shaw had not taken the racial promises of Civil War and Reconstruction lightly, and he was willing to make sacrifices and work hard for their fulfillment.

Not all black Tennesseans had the confidence and determination of Ed Shaw, but few viewed the Civil War with indifference. The years of bitter sectional conflict and political debate had cemented the connection between anti-slavery and war in the minds of all but the most isolated slave or free Negro. Many slaves genuinely worried for the health and well being of their masters under war conditions, but in the words of a young black preacher in Madison County, "the Negroes were praying to the Almighty to be set free." When the fighting actually came to Tennessee in early 1862, Louis Hughes explained that "I tried to catch everything I could about the war; I was so eager for the success of the Union cause." The negative trend in formal race relations during the pre-war years and the national controversy over slavery heightened a sense of group identity among black Tennesseans. Civil War would bring hardships and dislocation, but it offered promise and re-enforced hopes for freedom.

For most of the war, life for slaves well behind Confederate lines went on very much as usual. But Tennessee was never "well behind the lines." Black Tennesseans, especially slaves, faced an immediate dilemma regarding "loyalty" or "disloyalty" to their masters. Should they take advantage of reduced supervision and the presence of the Union army to revolt or run away, or should they continue to tend the fields, stables, and kitchens? Susanna, one of William G. Harding's 140 slaves at "Belle Meade" in Davidson County, rejoiced that none had "disgraced" themselves by running away in their master's absence. She maintained that the slaves' "true happiness consisted in doing their duty and remaining in their former condition." Most slaves, however, had not internalized the pro-slavery philosophy to this extent. Some remained loyal for personal and family reasons. George Knox, for example, postponed running away because a young lady of whom he was very fond cried and begged him to stay. Still others held to the security of a familiar way of life but used a growing labor shortage as a lever to win concessions from their masters.

Some blacks had little choice in aiding the Confederacy. In June 1861 the Tennessee legislature authorized the drafting of free Negroes for non-combat roles. Enforcement lagged, but a number of blacks served under this law. More importantly, however, hundreds of slaves were borrowed or "impressed" into service to build fortifications and perform other heavy laboring functions. With early Confederate military defeats and evidence of considerable mistreatment of slaves by the army, slave-owners showed a growing reluctance to part, even temporarily, with their valuable property. Furthermore, the virtual occupation of Tennessee by Union forces in 1863 encouraged blacks to act in support of their deep and long-standing desire for freedom. Those men and women who had professed loyalty and "sympathy for the south in order that they would not mistrust me" or who, only with "great effort," had "suppress[ed] their feelings of rejoicing" at Confederate defeats now abandoned their masters in great numbers.

At first the Union army tried to ignore the masses of runaways seeking its protective shelter, and the army moved only slowly "away from its policy of preserving slavery inviolate." But the word spread among black Tennesseans that Yankee soldiers did not have two heads and were not all rapists and plunderers as many of their white masters had warned. Consequently, Federal authorities found it expedient to make provision for thousands of black "contraband." "Disloyal" slaves now found new encouragement to make their bid for freedom. As one historian has noted, "the beacon of freedom all too often led them to the torments of poverty," but black Tennesseans readily surrendered "a guaranteed subsistence" for the chance to escape bondage.

Once a decision had been made to flee slavery, blacks had three basic alternatives. They could seek one of several contraband camps minimally maintained by Federal authorities and offering sporadic work opportunities. The could strike out on their own, risking recapture and struggling to survive by their wits, with but little money or property; or after 1863, men could enlist formally in the Union army.

Contraband camps, at best, served a transitional function. They provided fair protection from re-capture and acted as a buffer against the trauma of total self-support. But these camps had low budget and supply priorities. Newcomers arrived constantly, overtaxing the food, shelter, and medical resources, which had never been adequate. Sanitation deteriorated, and diseases such as smallpox were rampant. Stable employment was scarce and almost entirely dependent upon military needs. Black men chopped wood, repaired rail lines, and unloaded steamboats, while black women did laundry and worked in the hospitals. But Union soldiers frequently abused the blacks, forcing them to do their chores, impressing them for major work projects, and regularly neglecting to pay the legally required wages. As a result of these conditions, there was considerable turnover in residents.

Most contraband camps had been placed near or on the edge of Tennessee's towns and cities. These urban centers were administrative headquarters for Federal officials, but they also offered the greatest natural attraction to escaping or newly freed blacks who sought wage-paying jobs and a sense of anonymity. Consequently, as blacks became more secure in their "free" status, they moved out of the camps, often constructing "shantytowns" nearby. Practically every city had its black shantytown, and, as with Memphis' "South Memphis" and Nashville's "Edgefield," these communities became permanent. Therefore, while the contraband camps were, themselves, transitional, they served as an important urbanizing force among black Tennesseans.

Shantytowns are characteristic of refugee conditions in any society, and in Tennessee they were not solely dependent upon graduates of contraband camps for their population. Having no Federal camp nearby or consciously rejecting the dependency relationship fostered by the camps, thousands of blacks flooded urban areas. Here their dreams of personal freedom and self-sufficiency were severely tested by the perils of disease, crime, and unemployment. Some accumulated property and thrived. Others succumbed to forces which they could not overcome or control. Under even these conditions, however, the cities represented freedom from agricultural slavery, and the numbers of urban refugees grew throughout the state.

From early in the war a direct relationship with the Union army offered a third alternative to "disloyal" black Tennesseans. The army's presence in West Tennessee in 1862 encouraged this choice. At first General William T. Sherman sought to turn black contraband away, complaining that it was not in the best military interest "to set loose Negroes so fast," and ordered his troops "to have nothing to do with [them]." By the fall of 1862, however, army engineers had come to recognize the difficulties of building fortifications and maintaining open communication and transportation lines in enemy territory. Consequently, necessity caused even Sherman to change his mind, and black laborers were issued "clothing, food, and tobacco" and put to work. When army treatment did not meet black expectations and volunteer labor proved insufficient, impressment filled the ranks.

By 1863 the war had become a campaign of occupation and attrition, and manpower needs mounted. With the issuance of the Emancipation Proclamation, the Lincoln administration now felt free formally to enlist blacks in the army. Here they continued to perform a disproportionate amount of foraging and fatigue duty, but incentives eventually attracted 20,133 black men into the Army of Tennessee. The army opened recruiting stations in Chattanooga, Clarksville, Columbia, Gallatin, Knoxville, Lynnville, Memphis, Murfreesboro, Nashville, Shelbyville, Tullahoma, and Wartrace. And when Secretary of War Edwin Stanton made it clear in September 1863 that "all Colored Troops will forever be free," a great deal of black hesitancy about entering "another white-controlled authoritarian institution" diminished.

By October 1863 almost 4,000 blacks had enlisted in Tennessee. Many of these early recruits were former members of labor battalions, and engineering needs and white prejudices combined to delay for many months the acceptance of blacks as real combat troops. Black Tennessee soldiers were organized into separate regiments, with black noncommissioned and white commissioned officers. Discriminatory pay scales were in effect until June 1864, and black units usually operated separately from white units. Nevertheless, by early 1864, black Tennesseans had begun to earn respect as combat soldiers.

The largest number of black troops were stationed in or near Memphis. This location brought them into conflict with the forces of the former slave trader, now general, Nathan Bedford Forrest. Their most unfortunate encounter involved the so-called Fort Pillow Massacre—Fort Pillow being an outpost located on the Mississippi River, some forty miles north of Memphis. The dirt fort, garrisoned by less than 600 men, half of whom were black, was attacked on April 12, 1864, by Forrest's army of over 3,000. After a fierce fight and some confusion over a flag of truce, the Confederates stormed the barricade and proceeded literally to slaughter the black defenders and several members of their families living inside. The commanding white officer, Major William F. Bradford, was captured and executed in keeping with Confederate policy toward officers of "nigger troops."

Black soldiers fought General Forrest on several other occasions in the Memphis area, but their most important military effort in the state occurred during the battle of Nashville, December 1864. Over 15 percent of the front line troops involved in this two-day conflict was black, as was almost 20 percent of the casualties. General George Thomas, at first skeptical toward using blacks as combat soldiers, became a convert during the ferocious battle with General John B. Hood's Confederate Army of Tennessee. Thomas paid tribute to his black troops at Nashville: "The blood of white and black men has flowed freely together for the great cause which is to give freedom. . . . Colored Troops exhibited courage and steadiness that challenged the admiration of all who witnessed [their] charge."

Black military participation in Tennessee had been limited but significant. Not only had those black soldiers recruited in the state played key

roles in such crucial battles as that at Nashville and suffered grievous casualities as at Fort Pillow, but their sheer numbers were impressive. One historian has estimated that 40 percent of all black men eligible for military service actually enlisted. Furthermore, these 20,000 men also represented 40 percent of all Tennesseans who served in the Union army. Why did black Tennesseans give such strong support to the Union military cause when it brought curbs on their personal freedom, brought discrimination, scorn, and abuse from many white fellow soldiers, and left their families vulnerable to retaliation from Confederate sympathizers? Revenge undoubtedly motivated many, but most black Tennesseans had a more creative rationale. As one former slave answered his mistress's accusations, "No'm I ain't fighting you, I'm fighting to get free." By risking their lives, black soldiers were laying solid claim to meaningful freedom and "greater rights for their race after the war." Escaped slave and army teamster George Knox summed up black determination when he concluded that "if we had made our bed hard, we would lay on it, and never go back until we were taken or times were better."

White Tennesseans resented and feared black "disloyalty"; for them, the war was a white man's war and blacks had no legitimate interest in its outcome. The logic of this assumption had already been undermined, however, by the pervasive pre-war fears of slave revolt. If the exhortations of distant abolitionists might be expected to stimulate slave unrest, how much more catalytic would be the approach of Union troops? Perhaps surprisingly, black Tennesseans showed little desire for subversive violence, but their willingness to abandon their masters and seek the cities or actively to support the enemy was a direct affront to white racist assumptions and sensibilities. Even the Union-sympathizing whites of East Tennessee resented the influx of runaway blacks to towns such as Athens, Cleveland, Knoxville, and Chattanooga. But the keenest hostility of all came from Memphis, a community with an extremely large and volatile population of black refugees and headquarters for most black Union soldiers. An armed, uniformed, escaped slave was the ultimate psychological burden for whites to bear. Tennessee's towns were genu-

---

(*Above*): Battery A, 2nd U.S. Colored Light Artillery, Department of the Cumberland. *By permission of the Chicago Historical Society.* (*Below*): Confederate General Nathan Bedford Forrest's troops massacred black Union troops after storming Fort Pillow on April 12, 1864. *From Harper's Weekly, April 30, 1864.*

inely threatened by the thousands of impoverished and unemployed newcomers; the shantytowns and contraband camps were a menace to community health and safety. And yet the most dangerous and upsetting threat to white Tennesseans came from the general disruption of race relations. White Irishmen might now find themselves competing with black men for wages on the Memphis docks or parents of white children with no educational opportunities might encounter black children in Nashville attending free schools run by "Yankee schoolmarms." A poor white woman in Chattanooga expressed it best: "The town is so crowded with them we have but a slim showing. I want to go sum wheir wheir ther is no negrows . . . *it is so different from what it used to be*" (italics added). The war had given blacks an opportunity to cross the social barriers of racial slavery, and most had not hesitated to grasp it.

The war also created an atmosphere of uncertainty for the state's political institutions. The Confederate government fled to Mississippi in the face of Union victories in early 1862, and shortly thereafter President Lincoln appointed Andrew Johnson as military governor. For the next three years Unionists struggled to restore civil government to the state, and during these years, racial policies remained essentially in the hands of Federal agencies, i.e. the army and the Freedmen's Bureau. However, with the amendment of its own constitution to prohibit slavery in January 1865, the election of William G. "Parson" Brownlow as governor in March, and the acceptance of the Thirteenth Amendment in April, Tennessee was ready to be restored to the Union. After another year's delay and the ratification of the Fourteenth Amendment, formal restoration was accomplished in the summer of 1866. Now, as historian Paul Bergeron has pointed out, "once Tennessee was safely back in the Union, the question of who should rule the state became . . . critical."

Prior to this time, of course, thousands of black Tennesseans had already liberated themselves under the protective umbrella of Federal occupation forces. They remained dependent upon white politicians, however, for legal emancipation and guarantees of civil rights under the new laws. Progress on these matters had not come readily. Tennessee's Unionists, concentrated in East Tennessee, at first had denied any tie between emancipation and war. They hoped to coax reluctant Secessionists back into the fold and were very uncomfortable with the Emancipation Proclamation. The venerable Unionist, T.A.R. Nelson, even went so far as to endorse the Confederacy rather than accept Lincoln's decision. Continued Confederate resistance and military expediency eventually forced Johnson, Brownlow, and their supporters to give an unenthusiastic endorsement to emancipation and even opened the way for more than 3,700 blacks to enlist in the state militia. But when the constitution of 1835 was finally revised to abolish slavery, black Tennesseans gained little more than "free Negro" status. They could not legally sell merchandise, marry whites, or give court testimony against whites. They could not buy alcoholic beverages, and penalties for blacks convicted of crimes were more severe than for whites. Meanwhile, some municipal ordinances carried restrictions to still greater lengths.

From 1864 until 1869 Tennessee was governed by "Radical" Republicans. Their "radicalism," however, stemmed from their approach to Unionism, political reorganization, and the disfranchisement of "Rebels," and not from their racial attitudes. Beginning with the pressure to accept emancipation, they experienced an internal conflict between political loyalty to congressional policy and a desire to maintain clear racial distinctions in the areas of civil rights and social intercourse. Governor Brownlow, for example, tried to revive the old idea of colonization, and there was not a great deal of difference in Andrew Johnson's statement that he expected blacks to "stay in the same space in freedom as they did in slavery" and that of the avowedly racist and race-baiting Democratic newspaper, the *Memphis Avalanche,* which insisted in March 1866 that blacks were "still slaves in fact if not in name." The Radicals specifically feared that an expansion of black rights would lead to an influx of freedmen from more repressive neighboring states. They finally yielded to congressional pressure in May 1866 and extended all rights of citizenship to "Persons of Color" except the privileges of marrying whites, serving on juries, and voting. Without the security of slavery to maintain racial boundaries, the definition of "Persons of Color" was taken beyond the pre-war statement, so that it now included anyone "having any African blood in their veins." The legislature also made it clear in 1867 that the new public education bill did not "require the education of colored and white children in the same school."

Radical rule in Tennessee, however, faced a constant challenge from more "conservative" and conciliatory political voices. This contest left the Radicals vulnerable to black pressure for expanded participation in local and state politics. As early as the presidential campaign of 1864, outspoken blacks had called for suffrage as a meaningful corollary to emancipation, and they had held torchlight parades in Tennessee in support of Lincoln and Johnson. But these appeals, based upon logic and fairness, did not begin to pay dividends until they were accompanied by real or potential power. When the legislature failed to grant full citizen-

ship in 1865, blacks from across the state met in Nashville and petitioned Congress not to seat the new Tennessee delegation in Washington.
In turn, restoration was delayed until the state ratified the Fourteenth
Amendment. Nevertheless, suffrage for blacks was not granted by the
Brownlow government until 1867, when it became obvious that black
votes were needed to counteract growing Conservative strength in Tennessee. When the "Parson" decided to support black suffrage, he made
it clear why he had changed his mind. "We have two reasons for doing
this," he said. "The first is a selfish one; it is necessary for sixty or seventy thousand votes to kick the beam, to weigh the balance against reb-
elism." His credibility would have been saved if he had stopped there.
But instead, he went on to indicate that "the second reason is because it
is proper and just." "Proper and just" did not imply the right to hold office or to sit on juries until blacks gave their overwhelming support to
Brownlow in the fall election of 1867. In January 1868, the legislature finally removed these last two political disabilities. As Edward Shaw's
controversial career demonstrated, however, black leaders and voters
had not been as naive nor as passive in the process of political Reconstruction as many whites had expected.

Black Tennesseans recognized that an end to slavery had produced
many open questions, and they actively campaigned for answers. Since
virtually all power still rested with whites, blacks frequently found
themselves in a position of having to "appeal" for fair opportunity and
protection. Invariably they made their appeal on the basis of justice and
rights, and they tried to avoid encouraging a white predisposition toward paternalism. Slavery had been defeated, and furthermore, black
Tennesseans felt they had *earned* the full privileges of citizenship "by virtue of their [strong] support of the winning cause during the war." As
Nashville blacks argued in a petition to the legislature in 1865, the government could now grant "the colored man . . . a vote as safely as it
trusted him with a bayonet." Ignoring pre-war city ordinances prohibiting black gatherings, blacks throughout the state met to discuss their future as freedmen and to prod unenthusiastic white officials.

Slavery had denied southern blacks the opportunities to choose and
develop public leaders, but the campaign for freedom and citizenship
during the late 1860s pushed several individuals to the fore: among
them, Edward Shaw, Hannibal Carter, and Morris Henderson of Memphis; Randall Brown, Nelson Walker, and Peter Lowry of Nashville;
and W.F. Yardley, William Scott, and M.J.R. Gentle of East Tennessee.
These men were predominantly mulatto, either businessmen or preach-

ers, and for the most part had been "free Negroes" before the war. This early leadership elite often concerned itself with such local matters as schools and health services, but these men placed primary emphasis upon civil and political rights. Beginning in 1865 and continuing annually for more than twenty years, black political leaders met in Nashville to discuss racial progress in the state. The annual convention dealt with many issues, from murder to migration and from segregation to sanitation, but the prevailing philosophy among delegates over the years held that until full civil and political equality had been recognized, black Tennesseans would remain vulnerable and dependent upon white benevolence.

Although having to appeal to whites for public justice, blacks demonstrated a strong desire to improve their own position. As historian John Cimprich has noted, from their earliest days of liberty, former slaves in Tennessee "willingly accepted any aid which seemed to enhance their freedom, [but] always retained their independent-mindedness." A basic component of freedom for black Tennesseans was economic opportunity. Tens of thousands flocked to the cities in search of wages and employment, but most former slaves remained in the country. Here they sometimes took up residence on the abandoned farms of their previous owners or sought to rent land for cultivation. Lacking the capital to buy property at first, blacks entered wage and sharecropping contracts as expedient methods of gaining the necessary resources to achieve independence. Many held out hope that rumors of Federal plans to give each freed family forty acres and a mule from confiscated Confederate property would be true, but this was not to be the case. Instead black Tennesseans faced a white determination to continue exploiting the former slaves by refusing to sell them land and thus keeping them dependent upon white landowners. Talent, perseverance, and luck enabled some blacks to become substantial and successful farmers in spite of these obstacles, but most freedmen, especially in the old plantation areas of West and Middle Tennessee, still farmed the white man's land "with a white man's plow drawn by a white man's mule." In these regions where the black population was greatest, less than 10 percent of the former slaves had been able to purchase any land by 1883.

Basic education ranked second only to economic independence among the early goals of newly freed blacks. By 1863–64, northern missionary organizations such as the Western Freedmen's Aid Commission and the American Missionary Association had begun to work actively in the crowded contraband camps and shantytowns in Tennessee. Their focus upon education, however, had frequently been preceded by the efforts of blacks themselves. During the war, for example, blacks had conducted their own schools in Memphis, Springfield, Nashville, Columbia, Murfreesboro, Pulaski, and Knoxville. Few qualified black teachers lived in Tennessee, and the black illiteracy rate probably exceeded 95 percent. Black Tennesseans, therefore, welcomed white aid, whether it was private or, after 1865, from the Freedmen's Bureau. But they continued to support the schools with their own money and labor. In spite of white harassment and economic hardship, attendance grew at the black schools. If a school was burned, another was built; if no qualified teacher could be found, a local person often stepped forward. In 1865, Alfred Anderson of Knoxville filled such a teaching post because "I fealt that this pepel must be trained for I knew the wair humans. I sacrificed by bisness." Spelling was not important, as reading took highest priority in Freedmen's schools. Writing and arithmetic received some attention, but most black students concentrated either upon McGuffey's *Eclectic Reader* or the American Tract Society's new *Freedmen's Primer.*

In March 1867 the Brownlow administration enacted a law providing for free public education for all children in Tennessee. The state had no strong tradition of public schools, and many whites resented especially the social and financial implications of supporting black institutions. Therefore, under these circumstances the new state schools were malnourished and strictly segregated. Most black Tennesseans accepted segregation in education as inevitable and, perhaps, even desirable. Ed Shaw dissented sharply, however, arguing that separate schools allowed whites to discriminate financially in their own favor and, more importantly, that such policies attached a "stigma of inferiority" to black children. Shaw went on to argue that integrated schools would "hasten to destroy that school of prejudice . . . that teaches the colored child [that he or she] is inferior." Shaw's outspoken position did not reflect the opinions of a majority of black Tennesseans. Most saw even a separate system of education as an acceptable alternative to the pre-war practice of exclusion.

As a generally despised minority with little political, economic, or moral clout, blacks in Tennessee held a decidedly tenuous grip on freedom. While their political gains rested upon the shaky foundation of white Republican expediency, economic security had proven to be even more elusive. Bishop Isaac Lane remembered from his own experience that "our former owners prophesied that half of us would starve . . . [and] it must be admitted . . . that we had a hard time . . . but the harder the time, the harder we worked and the more we endured. For six months we lived on nothing but bread, milk, and water." But without land in an agricultural society, education, determination, and hard work could produce only limited results.

In fact, life and livelihood were always vulnerable. The race riot in Memphis during May 1866 made this very clear. This river city had become a mecca for blacks from throughout the Mississippi Delta and had also served as a major headquarters for black Union troops. Whites had become increasingly uneasy as the black population grew to over 60 percent by 1866, and the crowded community in South Memphis became both a symbol of southern military defeat and a frightening threat to traditional race relations. Competition for jobs and discriminatory enforcement of vagrancy laws focused these tensions, and on May 1 and 2 violence exploded throughout the city. By the time calm had been restored "two whites and 46 blacks [had] lost their lives. Some 75 persons were injured, 100 persons robbed, 5 black women raped, 91 homes burned, 4 black churches demolished, 8 black schools destroyed, and $17,000 worth of government properties lost or stolen." No whites were punished or blacks compensated for these outrages.

In addition to such spontaneous violence, the Ku Klux Klan terrorized black Tennesseans in a more systematic fashion between 1866 and 1869. Led by Grand Wizard Nathan Bedford Forrest, the Klan phenomenon appeared throughout most of the state, serving as a romantic pretense for nightriders to burn black schools, harass their teachers, and generally intimidate rural black families. The Klan opposed black political participation, land owning, and education—the basic tenets of freedom and citizenship. The hooded "order" also operated in the cities, and in 1868 marked Ed Shaw for "assassination." He and other black leaders armed themselves, and when attacked at a large rally of Memphis blacks, drew their pistols and returned the fire "with a rattling volley."

Federal pressure eventually curbed Klan activities, but blacks still had to live with considerable insecurity. They continued to fall victim to institutional types of violence. White authorities severely limited black service on juries and in a de facto manner maintained the pre-war policy of discriminatory punishment. In 1867, black inmates exceeded whites in the state's jails, and by 1877, their numbers were more than double that for whites. Furthermore, with the rise of convict leasing, some blacks encountered virtually a new form of slavery.

The Federal government made one significant attempt to offset the vulnerability of blacks and to facilitate their transition from slavery to freedom. In March 1865 Congress created the Bureau of Refugees,

Freedmen and Abandoned Lands, commonly called the Freedmen's Bureau. This agency operated throughout the South and had as its first responsibility the relief and protection of refugees. Tennessee had an abundance of black refugees since the presence of Union troops and the early collapse of the Confederate government encouraged slaves both from within and outside the state to run away. By the time the war ended, the Freedmen's Bureau had also become a "catch all" instrument for guaranteeing black freedom, supporting and expanding the educational work of philanthropic organizations, encouraging family relations and morality, and evolving a practical system of compensated labor to replace slavery.

Black Tennesseans clearly needed the support and protection of an agency such as the Freedmen's Bureau. In rural counties such as Hickman, Dyer, Weakley, and Haywood, for example, owners had refused to free their slaves until the end of the summer of 1865. More generally, the scarcity of urban jobs, extremely low level of literacy, and widespread white determination to keep blacks landless presented major hurdles to persons having few resources other than a dogged determination to survive and succeed. In response, Freedmen's Bureau officials in Tennessee set up a network of full and part-time agents throughout the state. These agents were sometimes native blacks, such as James C. Napier in Nashville, but were most often white army officers or newcomers from the North. Consequently, most southern whites resented their presence, and blacks received a heavy dose of Yankee paternalism and the "Puritan Ethic."

Blacks put much faith in the Freedmen's Bureau. They appealed to its courts to obtain unpaid wages and for relief from persecution under vagrancy laws, and they came in droves to the schools it supported. But white landowners also found bureau agents useful. No unbiased student of the period could fault the freedmen for a lack of determination to succeed, but they had gained one very important freedom and that was the freedom to say "no" to laboring terms offered by whites. Economists Roger Ransom and Richard Sutch have estimated that blacks in the South, by working less slavelike hours and reducing the hours worked by women and children, voluntarily withdrew one-third of their labor from the southern economy. This conscious decision and the natural disruption caused by increased mobility and urban living created a severe labor shortage in parts of Tennessee during the years just after the war. As a result, whites frequently turned with success to the Freedmen's Bureau to compell or influence black workers to sign wage or share contracts and return to the farms.

The full weight of the Freedmen's Bureau, however, was felt in Tennessee for only a short period of time. With the state's full restoration to the Union in 1866, the agency abolished its courts, and with the provision for free public education for all children in 1867, steadily reduced its expenditures on schools. Even during these years when blacks received the full thrust of the program, the results had been uneven. Money and attention had been concentrated upon the cities, and the bureau had been most assertive where the presence of Union troops was visible. In rural areas, agents made periodic reports, but black living conditions were determined most by their poverty and their white landlords.

By 1868 congressional enthusiasm for southern blacks had waned, thus undermining the appropriations and authority of the bureau. Its presence lingered in Tennessee until 1870, and it left a positive legacy in education after that time: a thin network of black elementary schools and a small number of higher educational institutions that, while terribly malnourished, provided the rudiments of education to a constantly growing number of black students. But in the area of economic reform and advancement, the bureau's decision to foster labor contracts upon blacks rather than make land available had fateful consequences. Blacks remained economically dependent upon whites and their transition from slavery to freedom was greatly impeded.

Following the defeat of slavery, black Tennesseans sought equality and equal protection in public institutions, but when rebuffed they hardly collapsed into social impotence. An absence of civil and political rights did not prevent a vital and important expansion in black institutions. Northern missionary organizations, for example, had founded a number of schools intended to train black teachers, preachers, and other leaders. Fisk University and Central Tennessee College were founded in Nashville in 1865. Roger Williams University opened its doors in the same city in 1867. In 1869 Le Moyne Institute began its long record of service in Memphis, and during the 1870s Knoxville College was founded in Knoxville and Meharry Medical School completed Nashville's outstanding quartet of black educational institutions. The only black-controlled school, Lane College, began instruction in Jackson in 1879 under the guidance of the newly independent Colored Methodist Episcopal Church.

The predominantly white faculties of these "colleges" discovered, however, that while hundreds of black Tennesseans turned to them for educational training, few had had access to the background preparation needed for advanced work. For many years, therefore, most of their curriculum involved elementary and secondary course work. Fisk had begun normal training in 1867, but not until 1871 did it become the first black school in the state to accept students into a genuine college program. The first class (four members) graduated in 1875.

Black colleges and universities had an immediate impact upon education in Tennessee; their trainees staffed a high percentage of the black elementary schools in the state. But religious philanthropy began to shrink after a few years, grants from the Freedmen's Bureau had disappeared by 1870, and financial survival became a major concern. The histories of how each of these institutions struggled to stay open during the difficult years of the late nineteenth century is replete with evidence of individual sacrifice, tremendous dedication, and stubborn determination. But the story of Fisk University contains the most dramatic episode.

In the fall of 1871 the Fisk Jubilee Singers went on tour. A small, "talented company" of student vocalists "had accidentally gathered at Fisk," and, leaving a financially bankrupt campus behind, they headed north in an effort to collect funds and win new friends for their school. The tour started slowly, barely covering expenses, until the group adopted slave "spirituals" as their format. Taking the name "Jubilee Singers" at this point, these Fisk students soon captured a wide audience in New England. Before they returned home, they also had performed before President U.S. Grant in the White House and earned over $20,000 for their college. The immediate financial crisis had been met, and a subsequent European tour in 1873 netted nearly $50,000, which was used to build Jubilee Hall on a new and much larger campus. Another important contribution by the Jubilee Singers, however, was that they formally had gathered together slave songs for the first time, taking this important legacy from the oral tradition of black America and preserving it and popularizing it for future study and appreciation.

Education was important, but the family continued as the basic social building block, although freedom offered many challenges to its stable and traditional development. The Civil War claimed the services of a high percentage of Tennessee's black breadwinners or potential bread-

---

(*Above*): The widely-acclaimed Fisk Jubilee Singers paused for this photograph about 1905. Their talent and effort earned important financial contributions as Fisk University grew in national status. *By permission of the Fisk University Library*. (*Below*): Blacks, separated from their families during slavery and war, expended great efforts to bring reunions. Advertisements such as these in the *Colored Tennessean* (Nashville), October 14, 1865, were common.

GOOSMAN TRANSFER CO.

winners, and, as war always does in any society, put a great social and economic strain upon the family. And yet, the war also opened new avenues for re-uniting husbands, wives, parents, and children who had been forcibly separated while slaves. Newspapers carried advertisements offering rewards for information concerning loved ones, and, for a brief time, the Freedmen's Bureau helped with expenses to facilitate reunions.

The rather chaotic and uncontrolled way in which slavery dissolved in Tennessee extended to most blacks an unaccustomed range of choices, mobility, and opportunities for excitement. The size and anonymity of the city encouraged the open sampling of previously forbidden pleasures of alcohol, gambling, and vice. Saloons abounded and even most grocery stores had bars in the rear where buckets of beer could be purchased for ten or fifteen cents. Intense crowding, poverty, and unemployment made family relations difficult. As many as six families might live in a single small dwelling, while others found "temporary" shelter in flimsy lean-tos or, in Chattanooga, sod huts. Rural life, meanwhile, resembled slavery for the landless blacks, and wherever they lived, black Tennesseans suffered a mortality rate more than 50 percent above that of whites. Given these conditions, neglect of wives, husbands, and children would be predictable. And, indeed, social problems were common in the black communities — just as they were in neighboring communities of poor and uprooted whites. Nevertheless, family values remained strong. Freedmen's Bureau and civil officials reported large numbers of weddings among former slaves, black men showed a clear desire for their wives not to have to seek employment, and parents took an active role in supporting education for themselves and their children. Most blacks settled their preferences upon brightly colored clothing and not the bright lights. Whites often criticized this penchant for gaudy dress, but it was a symbol of freedom and a compensation for the drab years of slavery that offered little threat to basically conservative black ideals and cultural values.

In addition to the family, black Tennesseans maintained and expanded the important community institutions developed within slavery. White social ostracism encouraged black self-sufficiency in churches and social organizations and, to a lesser extent, in business, the professions, and education. Before the war most blacks had attended white churches or were members of white-controlled denominations. With an end to slavery, mixed worship services became distasteful and uncomfortable for whites, and increasingly and unnecessarily inhibiting for blacks. Therefore, by 1866, black Methodists and Baptists in Tennessee were organizing separate black conferences and conventions, as well as separate congregations. Furthermore, the longstanding black denomination, the African Methodist Episcopal Church, organized rapidly in the state, attracting to its membership many of the more aggressive and assertive black men and women like Edward Shaw.

Religion had been important to slaves, but as historian Bobby Lee Lovett has pointed out, it assumed new institutional functions after emancipation. "Not only was school held in the church, but the teachers were often ministers or church missionaries. The important meetings involving black politics and movements for civil rights and suffrage always took place in the churches. . . ." Social life also centered around the church. Here black Tennesseans participated in suppers, picnics, fairs, festivals, and excursions. For a people who had few opportunities to travel, the low cost railroad excursion was very popular. A special occasion such as a church cornerstone laying, for example, might attract as many as several thousand people on excursions from nearby towns.

Social and fraternal organizations also played important roles in the emerging black communities, particularly as their activities promoted group effort and race consciousness. In addition to creating occasions for socializing, the fraternal organizations usually provided small illness or death benefits, represented blacks in public celebrations such as Fourth of July parades, and served as important training grounds for black leaders. National orders such as Masons, Odd Fellows, and Good Samaritans were active in Tennessee, as were local or independent societies such as the Nashville Colored Benevolent Society, Independent Pole Bearers, Sons and Daughters of Ham, and Daughters of Zion. Although refused recognition by their white counterparts, the Masons were the elite among the black organizations, but fraternal groups played such an important general role in the black communities in Tennessee that all "young men who aspired to advancement in public life found membership in these societies indispensable to their success."

In areas where money or prestige was involved, namely in business and the professions, whites showed a less dogmatic devotion to racial separation. White businessmen opened stores in black neighborhoods, and many whites preferred to have blacks dependent upon a few willing white lawyers, doctors, and dentists rather than accord professional respect to an individual of darker skin. Nevertheless, every black community produced a number of small, black-owned service establishments. Grocery stores, saloons, and restaurants predominated, but there were also barbershops, shoemakers, and livery stables. Most of these concerns were one- or two-person operations and thus offered limited employment opportunities in the communities. Some, however, were successful enough to provide owners like Ed Shaw the freedom to pursue a second career in politics or to lay the foundation for family fortunes such as that of black Memphis millionaire Robert Church, Sr.

In the professions, a few black lawyers, doctors, and college-trained teachers appeared in Tennessee at the close of the Civil War. These men were invariably trained outside the South or were virtually self-taught. In any case their numbers were insufficient to provide the rapidly growing needs of the black communities. In order to meet these needs, several of the mission-supported schools, particularly in Nashville, shifted more of their emphasis from rudimentary education to the training of professional leaders. Meharry Medical College, the law department of Tennessee Central College, and Fisk University combined to produce a small but well-trained cadre of black doctors, dentists, lawyers, and teachers in Tennessee. Their importance was illustrated when the earliest Meharry graduates quickly put their training to work fighting the recurring attacks of yellow fever in the western part of the state.

Some historians have seen the post-emancipation growth of black communities in Tennessee as a completely new phenomenon. The concept of black community, however, was not new; it had existed under slavery. The newness came as freedom provided blacks the mobility to gather in large, highly visible, *physical* communities and enough protection for self-sufficient black institutions to thrive in *public*. Their communities and their institutions soon produced a diverse and indigenous core of leaders. And, furthermore, the process of fighting to understand and guarantee a meaningful freedom not only re-enforced a common racial identity, but also provided most black Tennesseans with a common group of problems, frustrations and aspirations.

Outside the increasingly separate black communities, white Tennesseans insisted upon full control. By the decade of the 1870s, however, this dominance had been further defined to mean white conservative control. Politically, blacks had reached a peak of influence in the 1867 election. After that time splits in the Republican party and widespread intimidation by the Ku Klux Klan had reduced the numbers and attractiveness of black voters. In February 1869, Governor Brownlow resigned to take a position in the United States Senate, and in the fall election, Conservatives captured the state government. By repealing Radical legislation and abolishing local judicial and other governmental positions (including Ed Shaw's post as Shelby County commissioner), the Conservatives, soon openly referring to themselves as Democrats, "quickly won control from statehouse to courthouse."

Black Tennesseans did not have to wait long to discover what Democratic political control would mean for their already uncertain quest for equal citizenship. The new legislature immediately repealed Radical laws aimed at curbing the Klan and preventing segregation on the railroads. Furthermore, the General Assembly repealed the public school law and a law protecting the contracts of day laborers and house servants, and called for a new constitutional convention to meet in January 1870. The clear, if unspoken, intent for the new constitution was to roll back undesirable remnants of Radical "Reconstruction" and to fix a conservative, states rights, and white-dominated course for the future in Tennessee. The new document, ratified by the people of the state with a 3 to 1 margin, rejected pressure to disfranchise black voters but levied a poll tax on all voters and specifically prohibited interracial mixing in the public schools or in marriage. The Democratic legislature also moved to curb the exercise of one of black Tennesseans' most important freedoms — the freedom to withhold their labor. Growing black populations in the cities worried urban whites, and the mobility and unpredictability of black agricultural labor frustrated and antagonized large landowners. Therefore, in 1875 the legislature passed two pieces of legislation to curb these "abuses." A contract-labor law "prohibited anyone from enticing a laborer to break a work contract," and a vagrancy law made it a misdemeanor "to neglect to engage in an honest calling" or "to tramp or stroll" in rural areas without visible means of support. Meanwhile, the strong black desire for education had been temporarily thwarted by the repeal of Brownlow's public school law. County courts had done little to replace state funds, and black schools had practically disappeared. A new state school system was established in 1873, but educational opportunities for blacks remained discriminatory. In 1877, for example, only 38.6 percent of eligible black children was accommodated in the schools, as compared with 52 percent for white children. Therefore, although most black colleges were now doing some "college level" work, their elementary and secondary programs were providing educational opportunities which, otherwise, were simply unavailable to many black youths.

The political developments of the 1870s presented the most severe challenge to black optimism, and they did not go unanswered. On the state level, Democratic unity and general Republican weakness gave Tennessee's black minority of 25 percent few political opportunities. Locally, however, geographical districting still permitted blacks an active role. They ran and were elected as aldermen for example, in Knoxville, Maryville, Chattanooga, and Nashville and as constables and magistrates in Shelby, Maury, and Wilson counties. East Tennessee, where the Republican party was strongest and the black population least threatening, permitted the greatest opportunity for black office-holding. Here white officials in Knoxville and Chattanooga also approved the occasional service of a black man on jury duty. Local black officials were not content to be token representatives. Most participated actively in the governing process and used their positions to promote better municipal services in black neighborhoods.

In most of Middle Tennessee and throughout West Tennessee, however, Democratic strength predominated. And even in areas where a large black electorate might lead to Republican success, acceptable race relations required that whites harvest "the fruits of political victory." Ed Shaw and several of his black allies in Memphis never accepted this discriminatory arrangement, but theirs was an unending and difficult battle. Time and again, white Republican leaders promised major patronage appointments and future support for black candidates, only to renege after the black votes had been delivered. Shaw became bitter and denounced such betrayals, but he had no real alternatives. He kept up the fight throughout the 1870s, settling for nominations to minor offices, and gradually seeing his influence with the black masses decline as they tired of the fight.

With Democrats unified and in control of state government, black Tennesseans found themselves virtually "outside" the system. Without an effective voice in either party, they fell back upon the State Convention of Colored Men, held annually in Nashville after 1865. A vehicle also used by blacks in other states, the convention format allowed black Tennesseans to take a collective stand on issues critical to the protection of their rights and safety. In 1870 this convention sent a delegation, headed by James C. Napier, to Washington to petition Congress and President U.S. Grant for removal of the Conservative government and repudiation of the 1870 Constitution. Failing in this, in 1871 they asked Congress to establish a national school system and to pass special legislation to enforce southern (and thus Tennessee's) compliance with the Fifteenth Amendment.

The most controversial stand taken by the State Convention of Colored Men involved their unqualified support for Senator Charles Sumner's supplemental civil rights bill in 1874. A general measure intended to guarantee and define equal rights for blacks under the Fourteenth Amendment, the original bill took a strong stand against racial discrimination in public facilities and also against segregated schools. None other than Edward Shaw was chosen chairman of the 1874 convention, and under his leadership the body denounced Senator Brownlow for his opposition to the civil rights bill and urged its support by the state's Congressional delegation. The convention went on to give a specific endorsement to racially mixed schools, arguing that segregation encouraged a "spirit of caste and hate." An inferior black caste, however, was what most white Tennesseans preferred. And in the election of 1874, open black support of the civil rights bill drew angry fire from whites, especially in West Tennessee. In that region violence flared, with the worst episode occurring in Gibson County where sixteen blacks were taken from the Trenton jail and murdered on a road just outside of town. The civil rights bill passed Congress, in 1875, only after the "mixed school" clause had been removed.

During the 1870s blacks had managed to elect their first member of the legislature in 1872 and also to run an independent Republican candidate for governor in 1876. The legislator, Sampson W. Keeble of Davidson County, served only one undistinguished term, however, and the gubernatorial candidate, William F. Yardley of Knoxville, polled only 1 percent of the statewide vote.

Black Tennesseans resisted the deterioration in their status but found improvement hard to obtain. Federal authorities turned an increasingly deaf ear to their plans, the Republican party slowly abandoned its "southern strategy" and thus found it less expedient to court black voters, and the economic non-Reconstruction of the South left blacks heavily dependent upon unsympathetic whites for their livelihood. In short, black leaders who continued to fight for equal rights had very limited resources and little leverage.

Thousands of black Tennesseans turned to explore seriously an old alternative to their plight — emigration. In 1880 a short, weatherbeaten black man of seventy testified before a Senate investigating committee. He was barely literate, but his words were filled with emotion. "My people," he began, "for the want of land — we needed land for our children . . . was coming down, instead of going up . . . and I thought Southern Kansas was congenial to our nature, sir; and I formed a colony there. . . . We have tried," he went on, "to make a people of ourselves." The witness was Benjamin "Pap" Singleton, a former slave and cabinetmaker from Nashville. By 1880 Singleton estimated that he personally had led almost 7,500 southern blacks to Kansas. Perhaps one-half of these had come from Tennessee.

Singleton and other blacks, such as outspoken Nashville politician

Randall Brown, had begun to consider emigration as early as 1869. They received verbal encouragement from former Governor Brownlow and other colonizationists but never struck a very responsive chord among potential black migrants until the mid-1870s. At that time the combination of political, economic, and social grievances had dimmed black optimism. Singleton referred to a South dominated by "storms of sorrow and whirlwinds filled with fire," and the 1875 State Convention of Colored Men, to which Singleton was a delegate, gave more attention to the emigration debate than any other question. Speakers at the convention specifically cited the violence of the preceding year and the new Vagrancy Law as reasons for blacks to consider seriously their future in Tennessee. As with pre war colonization, however, emigration offered no real solution to the problems of black Tennesseans. Henry Carter, later a successful homesteader in Kansas, put his finger on a stark reality. When he asked a group of interested blacks at Nashville: "How many of you can put in your pockets $300 or $500 to go West with? To go on new grounds, where you get no returns for eighteen months?"

The vast majority of blacks in Tennessee could not or did not want to emigrate. At least for the next generation they would make the best of their Civil War and Reconstruction legacy. They constituted an economic "mudsill," and their civil rights hung precariously from white-controlled scales of justice. But for a few brief years in the early 1880s, it seemed that their *political* frustration might at last be coming to an end.

During the 1880 election campaign, Democratic party unity which had ousted the Radical Republicans in 1869 collapsed into heated debate over reduction of the state's bonded indebtedness. And, as Joseph Cartwright points out in his excellent study of politics during this critical decade, "this fierce internal battle among Democrats had an immediate impact on the way each faction perceived black voters." Both "state-credit" and "low-tax" Democratic factions ran gubernatorial candidates and this allowed the Republicans to capture that post for the first time in ten years. Republican Governor Alvin Hawkins, however, gave blacks little notice in his patronage appointments, and a significant number of black Tennesseans, led by the intrepid Ed Shaw, began to show public sympathy for the position of the low-tax Democrats. While most blacks re-

A group of black Tennesseans, following the leadership of Benjamin "Pap" Singleton, prepare to leave Nashville for Kansas in 1879. *By permission of the Kansas State Historical Society.*

mained loyal to the Republican party during the next few years, black support for the Democrats gradually grew throughout the state. For a brief period of time Ed Shaw, with the blessing of Senator Isham Harris, actually campaigned openly for Democratic candidates.

The factions within the Democratic party shifted from issue to issue during the early eighties, but their lack of unity had breathed new life into the Republicans. The Republican plurality, however, rested upon the loyalty of black voters. Using their new leverage, black leaders demanded and received more nominations to local offices than ever before and also managed to obtain long-sought party nominations to the state legislature. On fourteen occasions blacks were elected to the General Assembly between 1880 and 1888, led by Samuel A. McElwee's (Haywood County) three terms. The credentials of these men were strong, and they were active participants in governmental affairs — as were those tens of blacks elected to local offices across the state from Memphis to Chattanooga. In evaluating the contributions of the black legislators, Cartwright notes that they "challenged racial segregation in public transportation, fought for a fairer distribution of public educational funds, and attempted to halt economic proscription, lynching, and mob violence."

All direct political gains for black Tennesseans had come within the Republican party, but white Republican leaders had not made concessions willingly or comfortably. They continued to keep a disproportionate number of the patronage plums for themselves, and most resented having to depend upon blacks for their success. Furthermore, there was a growing hostility in all regions of the state toward the aggressiveness of black politicians and the high visibility of black officeholders. Even in East Tennessee, where token black recognition had been traditional, long-standing white commitments to paternalism and Christian duty were severely tested by the highly visible presence of blacks in *their* Republican party. When Democrats closed ranks behind Robert Taylor in 1886, sentiment grew in the Republican party for seriously reducing their dependence upon the black vote. Many white leaders felt that if they were ever to become a permanently viable and socially acceptable southern party, they must woo, instead, the new industrially-minded faction of Democrats. After 1886, therefore, the brief flowering of black political representation wilted rapidly under a barrage of new electoral laws and municipal redistricting. It was at this point that Ed Shaw withdrew from politics in disgust.

No black person served in the Tennessee General Assembly again until

1965. Slavery had not died easily, but after three decades, most of the debate was over, and a predictable pattern of race relations had taken shape. Not that it was very new or amenable to blacks, but it was clear. Emancipation opened many opportunities for black Tennesseans, but the former slaves "lacked the power to insure the permanency of their gains." As with antebellum free Negroes, they remained dependent and vulnerable. Reconstruction had been very minimal and of brief duration in Tennessee. At best, it had created confusion among both whites and blacks as to new social rules, regulations, and values. The rapid demise of the Freedmen's Bureau meant that the Federal government had shrugged off its responsibility for guaranteeing black equality onto the states. And by the 1880s Tennessee had shouldered this burden in such a way as to leave little doubt in the minds of its black citizens concerning the "equality" of their long-sought and hard-earned freedom.

3. The Burden of Caste, 1880s to 1920s

The young woman sank her teeth into the conductor's hand, braced her feet against the seat in front, and held a tight grip on her chair. Ida Wells had no intention of moving to the smoking car! The year was 1883, and Tennessee law required railroad companies to provide separate and equal first-class accommodations for black and white passengers. But to Ida Wells, a twenty-one-year-old black schoolteacher from Memphis, the crowded smoking car indicated by the conductor appeared neither first class nor equal to white facilities. Orphaned during the yellow fever epidemic of 1878, Ida had supported her five brothers and sisters by teaching near her home town of Holly Springs, Mississippi, before coming to Memphis in 1882. She wasted little time in making her mark in Tennessee. After being forcibly removed from the first-class coach, she left the train, returned to Memphis, and brought suit against the Chesapeake, Ohio and Southwestern Railroad Company.

Ida Wells lost her challenge to the railroad in 1883, but her determined resistance against racial discrimination and the failure of black Americans to enjoy equal protection of the laws had just begun. The campaign for racial justice became her career. In addition to her teaching duties, Ida Wells became editor and part owner of the *Memphis Free Speech* in

---

(*Left*): Ida B. Wells-Barnett in 1920. *Reprinted from* Crusade for Justice: The Autobiography of Ida B. Wells, *edited by Alfreda M. Duster, by permission of the editor and The University of Chicago Press,* © *by the University of Chicago.* (*Right*): Ida B. Wells-Barnett with her son Charles in 1896, four years after her brave stand against lynching forced her to flee Memphis. *Reprinted from* Crusade for Justice: The Autobiography of Ida B. Wells, *edited by Alfreda M. Duster, by permission of the editor and The University of Chicago Press,* © *by the University of Chicago.*

1889. She transformed this newspaper into a persistent and often strident critic of white discrimination and black passivity. In 1891, her editorial protests against the poor quality and low appropriations for black education in Memphis caused her not to be rehired as a teacher. She now chose to pursue journalism full-time, traveling widely and addressing black audiences up and down the Mississippi Valley in an effort to expand the circulation of the *Free Speech*. Soon, she and her newspaper had gained reputations which extended far beyond Memphis. Other black journals reprinted her stories and commented upon her editorials. And then in March 1892, there came a major turning point in Ida Well's career.

After a shooting in Memphis, involving blacks and police officials, three black men were taken from the city jail by a white mob and lynched. One of the victims was a close friend of Wells, and she immediately used the *Free Speech* to level a blistering attack upon the city which would "neither protect our lives and property, nor give us a fair trial in the courts." Wells followed her blast at Memphis with an investigation and general expose of lynching in the South. Local whites responded with verbal attacks on the editor's character and on May 27, 1892, while she was out of the city, totally destroyed the newspaper office and its equipment. Threats on her life, the ruin of her business, and the hostile racial atmosphere of Memphis convinced Ida Wells that she should not return. Instead, she moved to Chicago, where for the next thirty-nine years she raised her voice in uncompromising demand and protest over the denial of equal rights to black Americans.

While Ida Wells waited for her case against the railroad to come to trial, over 300 delegates from seventeen counties met in Nashville in 1884 to discuss the present condition and expectations of black Tennesseans. The keynote speaker for this twentieth annual meeting of the State Convention of Colored Men was James C. Napier, a small, light-skinned man whose impeccable conservative appearance complemented his serious and articulate address. Napier deplored the continuing racial injustices in the state, but he told his audience that their rights could best be assured by remaining loyal to the Republican party. He maintained that "with united purpose and concert of action" blacks could obtain more nominations to office and greater attention to their grievances. To lose patience or to flirt with the Democrats would only weaken their case.

James Carroll Napier. *Courtesy of the* Nashville Tennessean.

James C. Napier was the grandson of Elias Napier, the very wealthy white iron maker from Dickson County, and the son of a free Negro, who ran a livery stable in Nashville. James received most of his schooling in Ohio—first at Wilberforce University and then Oberlin College. During the Civil War he obtained a federal clerkship in Washington and thus began a long series of patronage jobs in Republican administrations. Napier returned to Tennessee at the end of the war, but maintained close ties in Washington. He had earned a law degree from Howard University and married John Mercer Langston's daughter Nettie, thus endowing him with close ties to the self-consciously "elite" segment of the black community in the nation's capital. Napier's economic, social, and educational advantages practically guaranteed him an early position of leadership among the largely insecure and uneducated black residents of the state. Napier was hardly dynamic in the mold of Edward Shaw or Ida Wells, but he was predictable, reliable, and non-controversial. He was elected three times to the Nashville City Council, served on the state executive committee of the Republican party and as delegate to Republican national conventions, and in 1911 was named by President William Howard Taft to the nation's most prestigious "black" patronage post, the register of the treasury. From these positions of influence, Napier argued the case for equitable treatment of black Americans, particularly those in Tennessee. He was a close friend of Booker T. Washington and shared Washington's faith in the gradual improvement of race relations. Napier helped found a bank to encourage saving among blacks in Nashville, sat on the boards of trustees of Fisk University, Meharry Medical College, and Howard University, and could be counted upon as a voice of moderation in any conflict between black aspirations and the restrictions of the caste system. When James C. Napier died in 1940 at the age of ninety-four, his eulogists cited him as a practical man and "respected" representative of his race.

By 1890 both Ida Wells and James C. Napier recognized the trend in race relations in Tennessee. The Civil War had ended slavery, and the rhetoric of Reconstruction had promised much to black Americans. Insufficient action supported these promises, however, and the restoration of conservative, white Democratic control soon made clear the limited terms of black citizenship. In effect, a racially defined caste system began to fill the void left by the abolition of slavery.

The legislature opened the way for this formal process in 1875 when it passed legislation allowing operators of public accommodations to reserve the right to refuse service to anyone in the same manner as "any private person over his private house." This act effectively nullified the Federal Civil Rights Act of 1875, and black Tennesseans who desired to challenge social tradition and seek equal access to public facilities and services now found legal obstructions in their path. Furthermore, specific laws and ordinances soon spelled out the demands for segregation or exclusion. Public education, of course, had been segregated by law since the new constitution in 1870. But in 1881, the legislature, over the strong objections of its four black members, passed a bill requiring railroad companies to provide separate first-class facilities for black passengers. Although such accommodations "were to be equal in all physical respects to those used by whites," a significant precedent had been established. Not only were private operators free to exclude blacks from their services, they could now be *compelled* to segregate their patrons.

The passage of Tennessee's first so-called "Jim Crow" law in 1881 by no means initiated the practice of segregation, but it provided a fateful rationale for racial separation. In the wake of the white backlash against black political assertiveness during the early 1880s race relations in Tennessee became noticeably more rigid. Prevailing white sentiment favored governmental regulation of interracial contact, and "separate but equal" offered a logic which even seemed consistent with the requirements of the Fourteenth Amendment. In practice, however, the principle broke down. Whites passed the laws, whites interpreted the laws, and whites enforced the laws. Under these conditions blacks had no assurance of fair treatment.

Black Tennesseans had never been able to exercise much power over state legislation, but coincident with the growing pressure for segregation, a series of suffrage restrictions in 1889-90 would virtually remove them from any serious political influence. These restrictions included precise registration procedures, a secret ballot, and a new and enforceable poll tax requirement. On the surface, these measures hardly seemed racially discriminatory, but in effect and in intent they had a disproportionately negative impact upon black voting. Illiteracy, mobility, and poverty were highest among blacks, and the new election laws took advantage of each of these characteristics. With no help allowed in reading and casting the secret ballot, a white interpretation of all registration qualifications, and careful personal record keeping required for registration certificates and poll tax receipts, thousands of black Tennesseans stayed away or were denied access to the polls. Historians Joseph Cartwright, Roger Hart, and Morgan Kousser have demonstrated convincingly the intent of the Democratic majority to reduce the black vote and thus undermine the Republican party as a serious contender outside of East Tennessee. But interested white contemporaries had made no secret of that fact. The *Memphis Avalanche* gloated when the elections in 1890 revealed that "the negro was practically disfranchised by the law compelling every voter to show his poll tax receipt before voting." And from Dyersburg came the report that "the poll tax and registration laws have played havoc with the colored vote." The racial effect of the new laws so nearly eliminated the black vote in the rural counties of West Tennessee that the back of the Republican party was broken in that region for decades.

Blacks responded to these formal expressions of a caste system in a variety of ways. Ed Shaw denounced them bitterly on the grounds that forced separation would imply black inferiority and therefore lead to greater civil and political inequalities. Ida Wells attacked the discriminatory application of justice head on: in the courts and in the press. And James C. Napier urged patience and continued trust in the federal government and Republican party. But to whom did black Tennesseans protest and what power did they have in their own hands? By the 1890s Congress had no interest in new civil rights legislation and little enthusiasm for enforcing old laws. The Civil Rights Cases of 1883 had dismissed a suit brought by a black Memphis couple against the Memphis and Charleston Railroad Company on the grounds that discrimination by privately-owned businesses was not prohibited by the Fourteenth Amendment. Then in 1896 the Supreme Court gave its sanction to segregation by upholding the legitimacy of the "separate but equal" doctrine. In 1898 and again in 1903 the Court refused to interfere with any suffrage restrictions that did not explicitly disqualify potential voters on the basis of race or color.

Given their political and economic dependence upon whites and also the fact that they accounted for less than one-fourth of the state's population, most black Tennesseans yielded to the odds. Some saw competitive advantages in a truly separate but equal society; others, with the memory of slavery still fresh, accepted even a caste system as a distinct improvement. When Ida Wells lost her teaching job for complaining about the inferior quality of black education in Memphis, she was dumbfounded by the general response of other blacks. "Miss Ida," they said, "you ought not to have done it; you might have known that they would fire you." Wells never gave up her uncompromising stand against inequality, but she learned in Memphis that most people would not take similar risks.

In addition to this popular unwillingness to resist openly the dictates of the caste system, a new generation of black leaders was emerging in the state. After thirty years of freedom, these men and women were no longer as influenced by the high expectations of the immediate post-war years, nor were they as focused upon the political arena for their credentials as "leaders." As ministers, fraternal officers, businessmen, or professionals, they had emerged as an elite within the lower caste and therefore carried a certain stake in its continued evolution. This leadership occasionally took major stands against inequalities within the system, but rarely did it challenge the system, as such. James C. Napier might carry petitions to the state legislature or Congress, deploring discrimination and asking for equitable funding for black schools or equal protection of the law, but when rebuffed or patronized, he took what he could get and waited for another day. Taking this line of least resistance hardly stirred the hearts or generated great optimism in the minds of black Tennesseans, but it enabled a person to meet the hardships and make the compromises of day-to-day living.

The new leaders did not surrender black claims to full American citizenship, but they articulated their positions with an eye to future achievement rather than immediate or short-term fulfillment. From Memphis, the Reverend S.N. Vass explained that "God is using the white man to bring us back to where we ought to have started, by excluding us from politics until first we receive some reasonable degree of education." And from Nashville, Professor W.H. Harrison of Roger Williams University advised young blacks that "if illegal discriminations are made, we must carry out our allegiance to the state, city, county and town, for God is not dead." Giving spiritual guidance to this public acquiescence was the authoritative national figure of Booker T. Washington, who greatly influenced the racial attitudes of black Tennesseans. Washington's emphasis upon education and his encouragement of black business enterprise had special appeal in Nashville. The capital city's postwar stability and the rapid appearance of important black colleges, universities, and church publishing houses allowed it to develop the state's most articulate black community (if somewhat less dynamic than Memphis). James C. Napier encouraged Washington to bring the annual meeting of the National Negro Business League to Nashville in 1903, and the prevailing sentiment expressed by black Tennesseans at that meeting was "self-help." There were concerns with continued discrimination, but R.H. Boyd, a Nashville business and church leader, conceded the practical fact that by leaving political and civic decisions in the hands of whites, blacks would be freer to "concentrate on raising [themselves] economically." Boyd had singled out the undoubted reason that most black Tennesseans did not choose to fight the formalities of the caste system more vigorously. When a person or group has few real economic assets, the struggle for survival and security takes priority.

Blacks who sought the cities as sources of greater freedom in employment often found little improvement over the rural life they had left behind. The range of job opportunities was somewhat greater, but unemployment, higher costs, and crowded living conditions endured well into the twentieth century. Manufacturing grew slowly in Tennessee, and firms employed few workers. Furthermore, in the larger operations, white laborers often refused to work with blacks. Textile mills, for example, hired only whites. By 1890, only 11,500 black men and women were employed in "manufacturing and mechanical industries" – a high percentage of these being found in the numerous iron foundries and rolling mills in or near Knoxville and Chattanooga. Consequently, most urban blacks depended upon uncertain and low paid employment in the service and building trades and as domestic servants. Daily wages for steadily employed breadwinners ranged from $1.00 to $2.00, but almost all food had to be purchased, and rent on two-and three-room houses varied from $6.00 to $12.00 per month. Housing shortages produced the lodger, and ten-year-old boys and mothers of young children frequently sought work in order to supplement meager incomes. In ageless fashion, ignorance, vulnerability, and unfamiliar dependence upon a money wage led to exploitation of blacks by loan companies and also to their being fined constantly by overanxious police authorities and justices of the peace. Loans advertised at fantastically low interest rates often included "balloon" contracts whose fine print reduced the black borrower and "his family to sleeping on the bare floor in a bare room after the loan shark had 'foreclosed' on all possessions" when the huge balloon or final payment could not be met on time. Disease and death plagued the

---

(*Above*): Black "roustabouts" provided essential labor, loading and unloading cotton and other goods at Memphis, a major cotton terminal for the Mississippi Delta. *Courtesy of the Tennessee State Library and Archives.* (*Below*): Most laborers in West Tennessee worked in agriculture, usually raising cotton on someone else's land. Here a black sharecropper poses with his white landowner, just outside Memphis, circa 1905. *Courtesy of Tennessee State Library and Archives.*

black neighborhoods to a much greater extent than for whites. They were the last places to get water and sewer facilities and paved streets, and they were invariably located in the low-lying areas where standing water was a problem. In Memphis during the years 1882-95, the overall death rate for blacks continued to exceed that for whites by 50 percent and for children under five by over 90 percent. The numbers of deaths declined during the early twentieth century, but the racial disparity actually increased in the cities of Tennessee.

In 1900, however, over thirty-five years after freedom, almost three-fourths of all black Tennesseans remained rural. Except for a few domestic servants, sawmill workers, miners, schoolteachers, and physicians, these men and women were farmers. A typical farm family included both parents, four children, and an occasional aged relative. Life was difficult. Housing varied, but for the majority it consisted of a small cabin constructed rather loosely of logs or slab boards. Having windows that were shuttered and rarely screened and only a fireplace or second-hand wood stove for heating and cooking, the cabins contained one or two crowded bedrooms and another room which served as a kitchen and living room. Sanitary facilities rarely existed. Household furnishings were sparse, consisting of beds (with straw, shuck, or cotton mattresses), oil lamps, a table and odd chairs, and a variety of cooking and eating utensils. Diet depended upon the nature of land tenure and the kind of farming involved. If the black farmer owned his own land or grew a variety of crops, his family tended to have balanced meals. But if he was engaged in one-crop tenancy or sharecropping (as most were), his family often subsisted upon fat pork, corn meal, and collard greens. Deficient in vitamins and other nutrients, this diet aggravated health problems and undoubtedly accounted for the prevalence of "stomach trouble."

Less than 25 percent of black farmers owned their own land, and over 70 percent were either sharecroppers or cash or share tenants. Regardless of race or status, however, farming during the late nineteenth century presented a real challenge. Between 1874 and 1897, cotton prices dropped to under six cents per pound and corn to under thirty cents per bushel. Gins and supply stores took their "cut" from this meager income, and after 1907, the boll weevil demanded a share. For sharecroppers this

---

Black workers "won" the jobs at hard labor — with little compensation. This phosphate miner toils in Maury County, 1914. *Courtesy of Tennessee State Library and Archives.*

condition was particularly perilous. One black Tennessean explained, "Dat's all dey is to expect — work hard and go hongry part time — long as we live on de other man's land." Rarely able to live on his "share," the "cropper" was forced to borrow from the white farm owner or merchant, and prices of goods bought on time averaged about 65 percent higher in Tennessee than prices of goods bought with cash. During the 1890s most farmers ended up in debt at the end of the year, but their families continued to treasure copies of Montgomery Ward and Sears and Roebuck catalogs, and a few special pages were preserved for ordering "a string of clothes" should a profit be realized.

Since they did not own land, most black farm families tended to be highly mobile. Assuming they could get out of debt, they often moved annually, making them ineligible to vote under new registration laws and disrupting the children's limited access to formal education. This mobility, however, was frequently curtailed by white enforcement of vagrancy legislation. These laws came into play when wages or cotton prices were too low to entice black farmers into voluntary contracts. In 1910, for example, Memphis police announced a plan "to clear the city of all vagrants and loiterers," and they were backed by the judge who promised that all persons arrested (most of whom would be black) should be allowed "to go free provided they [accepted] jobs offered by farmers" who were complaining of a shortage of laborers.

The cotton culture, involving over 50 percent of all black farmers in Tennessee and stretching eastward almost to Nashville, produced the lowest level of black landowning and was thus especially insecure. Occasionally it held unexpected rewards, as for Roman Cole, a black man near Jackson who plowed up $1,500 in gold coins in his cotton patch. Such a bonanza could hardly be anticipated by the thousands of other hard-pressed sharecroppers and tenants. Meanwhile, those black farmers concentrated in Middle and East Tennessee, who depended upon income and livelihood from hay, grain, and livestock, experienced fewer anxieties over basic sustenance. Their work was not as seasonal, more of their food was home-grown, and they depended less upon distant markets and unscrupulous merchants.

Still, rural blacks, East, Middle or West, faced major problems. At times they cooperated with similarly hard-pressed white farmers in an effort to overcome general agricultural depression. During the 1880s and early 1890s, therefore, the Colored Wheel and Colored Farmers' Alliance participated on the periphery of the larger and more influential white farm organizations. But as Roger Hart has pointed out, whites encouraged the black organizations only as long as they seemed to promote docility among the members. Blacks gained little from the highly publicized "farm revolt."

Tennessee gave itself a birthday party in 1897. Actually, it had been planned for the previous year, but the delay did nothing to detract from the grand and exuberant celebration of the state's hundreth anniversary. Historian Paul Bergeron has noted that the Centennial Exposition, held all summer in Nashville and visited by 1.8 million spectators, "stood as a dazzling symbol that closed the century on an optimistic note" for most Tennesseans. "The thirty years since 1870 had been 'a time to heal . . . and a time to build up.' The state had passed its time of testing and was ready for the new ventures of the twentieth century." But what did the celebration symbolize for black Tennesseans — almost one out of every four residents in the state?

Instead of being treated as a part of the mainstream of the state's history, with their contributions and progress displayed amidst those of James Robertson, Andrew Jackson, and other white citizens, black Tennesseans had their own separate exhibit hall. Furthermore, this building was located in that section of the park known as "Vanity Fair," a place "replete with strange people, strange sights, and strange noises." Here black Tennesseans took their place alongside reproductions of the streets of Cairo, a Chinese village, and a Colorado gold mine. By the end of the nineteenth century blacks had become a "special case"; expectations of full and equal partnership in the state's future had diminished. Whites had "passed the tests" of emancipation and reconstruction by replacing slavery with a racially defined caste system. "Niggertown," even more than the slave quarters, was becoming "a strange place." In the words of Evelyn Scott, a white novelist from Tennessee, "seeing Negroes at home . . . became unfamiliar to the point of picturesqueness. . . . It was a shock to realize Negroes possessed more freedom than a right to somebody else's kitchen, back veranda or rear garden!"

"Separation" was one thing, but even to pragmatic black Tennesseans such as James C. Napier and R.H. Boyd, the full phrase read "separate but *equal*." In this sense, the twentieth century did not begin optimistically. Throughout the South, state legislatures passed new disfranchisement and Jim Crow laws with the openly declared intent to push blacks into a permanently inferior and rigidly patrolled niche in society. Tightening the caste system did not create major problems in such autonomous institutions as churches and fraternities. In fact, these organizations continued to thrive, with Nashville emerging as a major publishing center for church literature among virtually all the major black denominations. In other areas, however, where law and caste etiquette made blacks dependent upon whites, conditions appeared less tolerable.

In 1905 the Tennessee legislature passed a law segregating passengers on streetcars throughout the state. Blacks from Memphis to Knoxville protested this extension of segregation as unnecessary and "an insult to the negro race." Calls for boycotts of the streetcars led to brief symbolic protests in Jackson and Knoxville, a court challenge from Memphis, and full-fledged attempts to provide competing black-owned transportation companies in Chattanooga and Nashville. The Chattanooga effort began with the formation of a system of hack lines that traveled on regular schedules between the city and the outlying black communities of Churchville, St. Elmo, Fort Cheatham, and Tannery Flats. Heavy patronage generated plans for replacing the horse-drawn hacks with forty-passenger motor cars, but after less than three months the enterprise collapsed from a shortage of investment capital and white legal harassment. In Nashville, however, strong support from virtually every prominent figure in the black community rallied the people to a successful boycott of the white streetcars during the summer of 1905 and cheered the appearance of motor cars owned by the Union Transportation Company in September. Black entrepreneurs such as R.H. Boyd and Preston Taylor invested several thousand dollars in this venture, and it was greeted with great enthusiasm by black Nashvillians. But their effort could not be sustained. The original steam-powered cars proved impractical, their battery-powered successors were damaged by the white power company that serviced them, and the need for reliable transportation in winter caused blacks to end their boycott of the white streetcars. Within a year, the protest against segregation in public transportation had faded, but black Tennesseans had not become indifferent. Randolph Miller, editor of the *Chattanooga Blade* and one of the forces behind the streetcar protest in that city, expressed a commonly held sense of exasperation: "They have taken our part of the library," he said. "They have moved our school to the frog pond; they have passed the Jim Crow law; they have knocked us out of the jury box; they have played the devil generally, and what in thunder more will they do no one knows."

Education posed a particularly thorny problem. The question of segregated public schools had been firmly settled during the 1870s, and in 1901 the legislature had closed a small chink in this caste barrier by extending the segregation decree to private institutions, as well. (The target of this legislation was the Presbyterian-supported college in Mary-ville. Black students had long been admitted to classes there, but by 1901, the numbers had become few and the treatment discriminatory.) But the questions of how much schooling and how "equal" the separate school systems would be remained open to discussion. The issues be-came critical in Tennessee during the first decade of the new century. At that time the Southern Education Board launched its attack upon the re-gion's general apathy toward education. As this agency's crusade began to pay dividends in the Volunteer State, blacks raised their voices in an effort to be included in the gains. The more assertive leaders agitated for equal advancement. The editors of the *Nashville Globe,* for example, complained in 1907 that "the inequality of the provisions made for the white and black children is too great at present. . . . In most of the af-fairs of the South, 'for the colored race' is synonymous with inferior ac-commodations. We hope that such will not be the case with the Nashville schools." Most black spokesmen avoided claims for equality, however, and appealed to white self-interest; a better educated black Tennessean would be a better worker, less inclined toward crime, and more alert to the problems of public health.

Many whites resisted the spending of *any* additional public funds for black schools. Senator Edward Carmack, who as editor of the *Memphis Commercial Appeal* had fomented the attack upon Ida Well's newspaper office in 1892, touched the quick nerve within the caste system: "They [education advocates] must say that the negro, however well educated, will be happy in the position assigned to him as an inferior creature . . . or they must say that the effect of education will be to fill him with dreams of perfect equality, the very thought of which fills the white man with loathing and disgust." Staying within the inferior station was more important than improving efficiency, morals, or public health. There-fore, while black educational opportunities did improve, they pro-gressed only at a very "respectful distance behind" white opportunities. In 1913, the average rural school term in Tennessee had reached 110 days per year, but for black rural schools it remained at less than 65 days per year. Less than one-half the black scholastic population of Memphis was in school in 1919, and one-third of those who did attend were with-out seats. And a 1927 study of the state's school system found that Ten-nessee spent $21.02 per year on each white child while spending only $11.88 on each black child. Without the additional work of such philan-thropic organizations as the John F. Slater Fund, Julius Rosenwald Fund, Anna T. Jeanes Foundation, and the General Education Board, combined with the enthusiastic support of a growing number of black Tennesseans, racial disparity in public education would have been much greater.

Another important aspect of the educational crusade in Tennessee had been the creation of a system of state normal colleges. For many years James C. Napier and other blacks had sought legislative funding for higher education, and when plans to establish three white colleges were announced in 1908, they began lobbying again with renewed vigor. The *Globe* publicized the issue widely among its black readers, and its editors, Henry Allen Boyd and Dock Hart, joined Napier, Preston Taylor, and others in an effort to mobilize black support and put pressure on the legislature. They made a convincing case, not only for the need for more and better black teachers, but also for a fair appropriation of federal land-grant funds previously used almost exclusively for whites at the University of Tennessee.

When a wide-ranging General Education Act emerged from the legislature in 1909, it contained provisions for three white normal schools and one Agricultural and Industrial State Normal School for Negroes. Semantics were important. If white taxpayers were to accept black higher education, the institution had to serve "a distinctly definite, different and important purpose," and "the courses of study . . . shall be of such practical nature as to fit the conditions and needs of their race." It was to be education with a difference. The "agricultural and industrial" part of the curriculum never flourished, however, and the emphasis upon normal training left the mission of the black school very similar to that of the new white colleges. But the difference remained, symbolically with the name and, more importantly, with financial appropriations. The original funding bill established a pattern which lasted for decades — $16,700 for the black school and $33,430 for each white school.

The General Education Act had not included funds to purchase or build campuses for the new colleges. Waiting for blacks began immedi-

---

(*Above*): The first faculty of the Tennessee Agricultural and Industrial Normal School, 1912. Principal William Jasper Hale is at front row, center. *Courtesy of the Bureau of Public Relations, Tennessee State University.* (*Below*): Bethlehem House (picture circa 1923) in Nashville offered training for black social workers and served as a stimulus for neighborhood improvement efforts. *Courtesy of United Methodist Neighborhood Centers, Nashville.*

ately. Cities and towns throughout the state offered land and authorized
bond issues as they competed for the white schools, but they shied away
from the black college. Although 50 percent of the state's black population lived in West Tennessee, no serious proposal came from that region.
The problem was race, and the major obstacle was money. Black leadership was the key to overcoming these obstacles, and it was only after tremendous organizing efforts by such men as Napier, Boyd, Taylor, and
Hart in Nashville and William Jasper Hale in Chattanooga that these
two cities made modest bids for the new black college. Nashville was
chosen, but all was not lost for the indomitable W. J. Hale. The state su-
perintendent of education named Hale "principal" of the new school,
and he served at this post (later as "president") from 1911 until his retire-
ment in 1943. Hale became an influential figure in the black communities of Tennessee, but he pursued a conservative racial path, preferring
to accept "half-loaf" appropriations rather than to complain aggressively and risk loss.

Black Tennesseans lacked the leverage to make effective protest
against segregation and unequal appropriations, but this impotence did
not foreclose black initiative. They were not simply content to be acted
upon by white society. Blacks continued to prod white officials for some
acknowledgment of such needs as "juvenile justice," instead of continuing the traditional practice of placing ten-and eleven-year-old offenders
in prison with adults. And they campaigned for the rudiments of public
health care, the presence of libraries, and the creation of parks in their
previously neglected communities. But in the spirit of the "progressive
era" of which they were a part, black Tennesseans also took positive action to improve their own communities and to stimulate efficient economic growth.

The thrust for community action came from the small urban middle-
class. Articulate, often well read, and with a self-conscious stake in society, these middle-class blacks adopted the reform rhetoric of the age. Invariably calling themselves "progressive Negroes," they gave birth to a
full spectrum of Negro betterment leagues, progressive Negro fairs, and
home improvement clubs, each supporting what it termed "progressive
lines of thought." In Memphis, efforts focused upon an orphanage, a
working girls home, and the creation of new parks; Chattanooga
stressed health and housing improvements; and Knoxville blacks pursued a varied program which included better school attendance, development of a YMCA and expanded park facilities. Nashville, however, with
its sizeable black professional class, experienced the most active pro-

gressive impulse. Neighborhood associations, women's clubs, and the Negro Board of Trade led numerous campaigns to make residential and business districts more attractive, to convince parents to provide greater moral guidance to their children, and to encourage the development of park, library, and YMCA facilities for blacks.

Giving aid, advice, and stimulation to the progressive efforts of black Nashvillians was George Edmund Haynes. A thirty-year-old Fisk University graduate and native of Pine Bluff, Arkansas, Haynes joined the Fisk faculty as associate professor of sociology and economics in 1910. He was a founder of the National Urban League and developed a training school for black social workers at Fisk. He incorporated his training methods into the social science curriculum and worked in conjunction with Bethlehem House, a black-operated training center financed by the Woman's Council of the Methodist Episcopal Church, South. Haynes's social workers encouraged domestic efficiency and good health and hygiene practices in the black slums, served in such social emergencies as that created by the city's disastrous fire in 1916, and also sponsored wide-ranging recreational programs for black youth.

The emphasis upon uplift and improvement through self-help also gave support to another phenomenon of the caste system—black businesses and especially black financial institutions. Almost all black-owned businesses in Tennessee were small and restricted by location and social pressure to black customers. A business which thus relied solely on the patronage of an economically marginal neighborhood had a future as precarious and vulnerable as its patrons. From time to time black businessmen and other leaders supported two approaches to upgrading the status of these enterprises. Most popular was the appeal to "buying black." In the words of the *Nashville Globe,* "we owe it to ourselves to strive with all the power within us to keep our little business enterprises alive." But it was difficult for the small black business to compete with the better financed white competitor, and it was here, argued many blacks, that their own capital-producing institutions should come into play. Tennessee gave birth to four black banks between 1904 and 1910, and each of these institutions expressed its desire to "set in motion business enterprises." The function of these banks in their respective black communities (two in Nashville and two in Memphis) varied during the next two decades, but they played important roles. The One-Cent Bank in Nashville, for example, was guided by the conservative financial views of James C. Napier and R.H. Boyd and, therefore, stressed "systematic saving among our people" and the building of confidence in race

institutions. The Solvent Bank of Memphis, however, was founded by one of the most successful black businessmen in the nation, Robert "Bob" Church, Sr. Church and his partners put their emphasis upon the more traditional banking goals of money-making and business expansion. Within the continuing economic limitations of the caste system, all four banks made a significant contribution to the efforts of black Tennesseans to expand their opportunities during the early years of the twentieth century.

World War I presented both challenges and opportunities to blacks in the South. They were called upon to send their sons and husbands to the army, to buy war bonds, and to plant "victory gardens." Black Tennesseans responded loyally and vigorously to these appeals, but most viewed their support as more than expressions of patriotism and national loyalty. Speakers at black rallies, time and again, referred to their expectations for improved race relations after the war. James A. Jones, presiding elder of the A.M.E. Church in Nashville, explained that "we hope that this war may serve to lift the scales from the eyes of prejudice-ridden America, and that the part we take in this fight will accomplish the required result, making the democracy of which we so much boast be a reality and not a mockery." Even J.C. Napier, speaking in 1917 as Booker T. Washington's successor to the presidency of the National Negro Business League, commented that if black support for the war effort did "not entitle us to a fair chance in the race of life, pray tell us what any set of people ever had done or can do to win that chance."

Expanded economic opportunities, however, offered more tangible short-term gains to blacks. In response, Tennessee's black population became even more mobile as poverty-stricken farm tenants, displaced miners, underpaid domestics, and low-wage industrial workers looked optimistically to the Du Pont powder plant at Jacksonville (Old Hickory), the Alcoa aluminum operations near Maryville, and the numerous war industries in Chicago, Cincinnati, Pittsburgh, and Wheeling, West Virginia. The Du Pont operation created by far the largest single wartime demand for black labor, drawing recruits from as far away as New Orleans and employing over 10,000 blacks by late 1918. Most black employees at Du Pont and Alcoa served as construction laborers, janitors, or semiskilled workers in the hottest, dirtiest, or most dangerous indus-

Health clinic being conducted at Bethlehem House, circa 1923. *Courtesy of United Methodist Neighborhood Centers, Nashville.*

OVER A MILLION DOLLAR RECORD

The One-Cent Savings Bank of Nashville, Tennessee, Shows Splendid Gains Through Conservative Management

LIKE the ROCK GIBRALTAR

Gigantic Financial Institutes Located Here

A BANK OF NATIONAL REPUTATION

THOSE WHO DESIRE AN INVESTMENT SHOULD CALL AT THE
BANK, OR PHONE MAIN 1851.

trial processes. Nevertheless, the wages were attractive and the new opportunities caused labor shortages among many traditionally "Negro jobs." When black Tennesseans chose to leave the state in search of better wartime employment, they generally followed a railroad route previously taken by a relative or acquaintance. Most traveled independently as single men and women or, in some cases, with their families, but others were recruited in groups by labor agents. An agent for the Wheeling Molding Foundry, for example, went to Chattanooga on several occasions and, by early 1917, had taken back more than 150 black laborers. Chicago was also a favorite destination, and it was a common expression among East Tennessee blacks that "any day you go to the corner of 35th and State Streets in Chicago, you will see someone from Knoxville if you wait long enough."

Despite the many displays of black loyalty, World War I was also a time of racial tension in Tennessee. Blacks had always lived under the shadow of violence, but their broadening pattern of urban migration combined with general war fears to put severe strains on the traditional relationships of the caste society. Whites complained constantly of streetcar congestion and of shortages of farm laborers and domestic servants. Overt white violence had been on the decline in the state for some time, but beginning in May 1917 and continuing for two and one-half years, Tennessee's racial climate exploded into a spate of hangings, burnings, and rioting. During that period, six reported lynchings and a small riot took the lives of at least seven blacks and threatened the safety of the entire black population of the state. White officials further complicated race relations by discriminatory enforcement of vagrancy laws and general harassment of black citizens in an effort to meet unskilled labor needs.

Ironically, the race riot occurred in Knoxville, a city with perhaps the strongest record of white paternalism and interracial peace. On August

---

(*Above*): The One-Cent Savings Bank and Trust Company, now called the Citizens Bank, was founded in Nashville in 1904 and is the oldest continuously operating black bank in the United States. Nashville Globe, *December 15, 1911*. (*Below*): The Solvent Savings Bank and Trust Company in Memphis figured prominently in the black business expansions of the 1910s and 1920s. Founded by Robert R. Church, Sr. in 1906, it was the second oldest black bank in Tennessee. *Courtesy of Roberta Church.*

30, 1919, a white mob had stormed the jail in an effort to take custody of (and most certainly lynch) a black man accused of murdering a white woman. Finding that the man had been moved, the mob destroyed the jail, looted nearby stores in search of guns, and headed toward the black section of town. Blacks put up resistance, and the national guard (camped nearby in Fountain City) finally restored order after several hours of conflict. At least one black man was killed, and it is probable that other deaths went unreported. Furthermore, after the riot, the black community was confined, searched, and generally harassed by the hostile soldiers. Although thirty-six whites were arrested during the fray, the all-white jury refused to grant any convictions. In effect, the mob violence had originated in the white community, among white citizens, but had buried itself in the harassment of blacks.

Black reactions to the violence in Tennessee ran from fear to indignation to organized efforts to reduce tensions and improve race relations. They petitioned the governor for better protection under the law and worked in local communities with white members of the Tennessee Law and Order League. The league had been founded in 1918 in an effort to arouse greater public sentiment against violence, and blacks particularly hoped to reduce inflammatory newspaper reporting of crimes allegedly committed by blacks. Editorials might denounce lawlessness, but these opinions were frequently offset by lurid front-page stories. Violence did subside and the Law and Order League gave way in 1920 to the white-controlled, but biracial Commission on Interracial Cooperation. Conservative blacks such as Napier and W.J. Hale participated in the commission's work, and it did play a role during the 1920s and 1930s in preventing a repeat of the concentrated outburst of wartime and post-war violence.

Many black Tennesseans, tired, frightened, or fed-up with their vulnerable status, simply joined the continuing exodus from the state. Black flight following extreme white violence was not a new phenomenon in Tennessee. Ida Wells had urged members of her race to leave Memphis after the trouble in 1892, and she specifically recommended the opportunities to be found in the newly-opening Oklahoma Territory. Several hundred Memphis blacks accepted Wells' advice, and after the public lynching of a black man in Chattanooga in 1906, the two black lawyers involved in the victim's case took their families and also resettled in Oklahoma. Long-standing ties of home and kin were hard to break, but the combining "pull" of economic improvement and "push" of caste-related abuses actually reduced the total black population of the state by 4.5 percent between 1910 and 1920 and continued to send a stream of black migrants northward and westward for the next fifty years (see Appendix).

The "normalcy" of the twenties included a return to a more stable interracial climate in Tennessee. But for blacks, all was not the same. Public violence declined and educational opportunities continued to improve, but the gains expected from the "War for Democracy" failed to materialize. Caste discriminations remained firmly in place, economic opportunities continued to be marginal and insecure, and persistent white hostility revealed itself in the form of a new version of the Ku Klux Klan. The collapse of cotton prices in 1920 seemed to justify a growing black pessimism toward a future based primarily upon agriculture. A small amount of money from new programs conducted under the Smith-Lever and Smith-Hughes acts reached black farmers in the state, but in the eyes of most black Tennesseans, farm conditions again appeared to have stabilized on the old low-price, sharecropper basis. The exodus from the farms continued. Bankruptcy, abandonment, and voluntary sale reduced the number of black farmers who owned their own land by more than 25 percent between 1900 and 1930, and the total black rural population fell by 15 percent. The number of blacks living in Tennessee's towns and cities, meanwhile, almost doubled during those same years.

The pushing and pulling forces of the war years had given many black Tennesseans new impetus to pursue the promises so strongly associated with American citizenship. Their pursuit did not end with the war, and it most certainly implied a willingness to break with traditional attachments to the land or region. Among the thousands of black residents who had left and would continue to leave the state were the more creative talents—men like blues composer W.C. Handy, former Jubilee Singer and internationally acclaimed tenor Roland Hayes, and the brilliant author Richard Wright and women such as Ida Wells and civil rights leader Mary Church Terrell. They found little flexibility for expressing themselves within the rigid racial code of the South. Similarly, ambitious young blacks seeking careers in fields such as engineering, law, and medicine found the prospects better in the North. This "brain drain" deprived the state of some of its best talent and leadership.

Among the overwhelming majority of blacks who stayed in Tennessee, the hardships of day-to-day living continued to absorb most of the energy that might have been used to force change and smothered all but the most persistent voices of protest against discrimination. Urbanization, however, had created a more dynamic *potential* in the black communities, and on those occasions when effective leadership did come forward, black Tennesseans showed a willingness to respond. They formed branches of the National Association for the Advancement of Colored People (NAACP), supported the growth of black businesses (including a chain of cooperative grocery stores in Memphis), took pride in the expansion of Tennessee A. & I. State Normal School, and concentrated their remaining political influence upon key local elections.

The suffrage restrictions of the late nineteenth century had eliminated blacks from statewide political consideration, primarily by disfranchising the rural black vote in Middle and West Tennessee. Republican gubernatorial support in heavily rural and predominantly black Fayette County, for example, declined from 1,050 votes in 1888 to 339 in 1894 and to 3 in 1906. In the cities, however, blacks had greater access to education, were less vulnerable to intimidation, and benefitted more from the strength and support of the "group." They had little chance of electing members of their own race to office, but when mobilized by able leaders they formed a critical voting bloc that demanded white political consideration.

Foremost among black political leaders was Robert Church, Jr., of Memphis. In 1916 Church presided over the formation of the Lincoln League, a black political organization active throughout West Tennessee but concentrated in Memphis. Black voters were still loyally Republican in state and national politics, but in local elections the Lincoln League took a pragmatic view. Church and his lieutenants demonstrated that they could deliver several thousand registered black voters to the polls and used this lever to extract campaign promises from the candidates. Better police and fire protection, patronage jobs, new schools, paved streets, sewers, and parks for the black community were negotiated. White politicians sometimes reneged on their promises to blacks, but Church used his political muscle to convince Edward H. "Boss" Crump,

---

(*Above*): Robert R. Church, Jr., became a powerful black political leader in the 1910s and 1920s. He is shown here in his Beale Street office, flanked by photographs of prominent national Republican leaders who praised his organization of black voters in Tennessee. *Courtesy of Roberta Church.* (*Below*): The Lincoln League dominated Republican politics in Memphis during the late 1910s and 1920s. This photograph was taken at a 1916 meeting of the league in Church's Park. *Courtesy of Roberta Church.*

the most powerful of all white Memphians, that he should avoid antagonizing such a large and potentially useful portion of the electorate. Basic caste discrimination could not be removed in this fashion, but Memphis blacks won many tangible concessions.

The two most specific and noteworthy examples of black political activism, however, came from Chattanooga and Memphis during the Ku Klux Klan campaign of 1923. The new Klan had ventured into the world of local city politics, and municipal elections in those two cities centered upon a complete slate of Klan nominees. By virtue of an almost unprecedented turnout of black voters, the Klan city commission candidates in Chattanooga went down to defeat. Their nominee for city judge won anyway, and it was acknowledged by all sides that only the black vote prevented the hooded order from taking complete control of the city government. Meanwhile, at the other end of the state, Memphis blacks used their organized political clout in similar fashion. As in Chattanooga, the Klan, facing a solid black vote, was narrowly defeated. In that election, however, Robert Church received several promises to the black community, which were not fulfilled. Therefore, when the anti-Klan mayor (Rowlett Paine) sought re-election four years later, he encountered strong opposition from the Lincoln League and lost to its and "Boss" Crump's candidate, Watkins Overton.

In Nashville, Knoxville, and other parts of the state the black vote was generally ineffective and apathetic during the 1920s. But Robert Church and thousands of black Memphians had shown that when strong leadership emerged, racial solidarity could be sustained in spite of caste restrictions and white hostility.

Sixty years after emancipation, black Tennesseans still found it easier and safer to accommodate with white-imposed standards of conduct, but seeds of change had been sown. The attitudes and expectations of the rising generation—more mobile, better educated, and free of first-hand memories of slavery—differed significantly from those of their more patient and dependent Reconstruction-era parents.

A protracted conflict between the students and administration at Fisk University during the 1924–25 school year revealed these differences, and, for those who might have taken notice, the clash foretold much more extensive unrest in the future. By 1900 Fisk had become one of the two or three most outstanding black colleges in the nation. Its graduates served in professional capacities in virtually every state in the nation. In Tennessee, other black schools were also making valuable contributions. Lane and LeMoyne had upgraded their curriculums, and most of the older schools now maintained small but legitimate college classes. But only Fisk was to earn class A accreditation. By the 1920s, however, the missionary-minded founders of institutions like Fisk University had died, and their replacements were men of a different spirit. Instead of preparing young blacks as equal, participating citizens, the new administration at Fisk, led since 1915 by white President Fayette Avery McKenzie, reflected the gradualist and accommodating approach of Booker T. Washington. James C. Napier's election to the Board of Trustees also indicated a conservative approach to black advancement. After 1920, however, student complaints at Fisk had become numerous. They complained of dress codes, abolition of student publications and student government, censorship of debates, and denial of the right to form a chapter of the NAACP. But at the heart of their unrest lay the question of whether Fisk University was to be a "Negro College" or a college "for Negroes" run by whites.

These young black Tennesseans (the overwhelming majority of the students were from Tennessee) sought more black participation in all phases of their education and less white paternalism, even if it meant the loss of some white financial support. After several preliminary protests, Fisk students staged an open demonstration against McKenzie's policies in February 1925. He responded by calling upon Nashville's police (all white) to quell the disturbance and arrest student leaders. The student body, in turn, went on strike. For over two months the school's policies and personnel were the center of verbal clashes between the black and white communities in Nashville, between alumni and trustees, and between students and administrators. Finally, in April, McKenzie resigned, and the campus slowly returned to normal. Strikers were restored to their previous academic status, and the new president, Thomas E. Jones, and his staff greatly expanded student autonomy in the nonacademic life of the University.

The students at Fisk, the members of Robert Church's Lincoln League in Memphis, and even a small group of followers of Marcus Garvey in Chattanooga indicated that by 1930, Tennessee's caste system may have dominated life, but it had not squeezed all the initiative from blacks.

Although a significant thread of protest survived, periodically sending bubbles from its fermentation to burst upon the generally peaceful surface, most black Tennesseans of the early twentieth century took the advice of James C. Napier and Booker T. Washington rather than that of Ida Wells. They accepted accommodation as a realistic temporary alternative to racial conflict. But accommodation, whether it was conscious or merely apathetic, molded white attitudes, black expectations, and race relations and decisively influenced the future course of social development in Tennessee.

Black Tennesseans may have looked upon the caste system as temporary, "yet," as the black writer Langston Hughes once observed, "how heavily the bricks of compromise settle into place!" The discriminatory "half-loaf" appropriations given the Tennessee Agricultural and Industrial State Normal School, for example — appropriations for which blacks "rejoiced" and were "exceeding glad" — set a precedent that for decades left the black school as the stepchild of the state's higher education system. In race relations, the willingness to accept segregation reinforced a practice of discrimination that gave ground ever so slowly. Furthermore, the Great Depression fell upon black Tennesseans with a vengeance. Facing its physical and spiritual onslaught, black Tennesseans were over 50 percent urban, almost double the figure for 1900, but they still stood on the bottom rung of the economic ladder. Overcrowding, disease, debt, and job insecurity offered few tangible advantages over the fear, hard work, lien entanglements, and economic backwardness of the Reconstruction-legacy tenant farm. The black worker was easily dislodged by those forced down the scale from above, and his position remained the most precarious and marginal one in the state's economy.

Langston Hughes went on to ask, "For bread, how much of the spirit must one give away?" "Bread" was still vulnerable for black Tennesseans in 1930, and for most, the "spirit" was hesitant. Eventually, however, still another generation of leaders emerged, a generation not unlike the Fisk students of 1925 but prepared by another world war, a technological revolution, and a continuing urban crisis to make the necessary break with the habits of compromise and dependence.

4. The Forces of Change, 1920s to 1970

Viola McFerren returned home from a meeting of The Original Fayette County Civic and Welfare League, tucked her two-year-old twins into bed and waited for her husband John to arrive. He came in exhausted and quickly fell asleep. Viola, however, did not doze. In recent weeks their home had been a target for rocks, and numerous phone calls had threatened the family with firebombing and murder. Somehow, she felt that by staying awake she might prevent an attack or, at least, warn the others in time to escape serious injury.

Until 1959 the McFerrens had lived the relatively anonymous life of a young black couple trying to earn a meager existence from a small farm in one of the four poorest counties in the United States. But in that year, qualified blacks had attempted to register as voters in Fayette and neighboring Haywood counties. Although approximately two-thirds of the population was black, few blacks had voted in these counties since the passage of suffrage restrictions in 1889–90, and in recent years virtually none (none *at all* in Haywood) had been allowed even to register. In spite of Viola's fears and hesitation, John McFerren took an active role in the registration campaign. Seeing his determination, she too decided to join the effort—a decision reached partly by the force of her own personal commitment and yet less consciously, also as a representative of a generation of black Tennesseans whose time for action had arrived. This irresistible combination surfaced in other black communities, as well, and produced dramatic results in Tennessee during the next decade.

Viola McFerren came to Tennessee out of necessity and chose to make it her home. As a child born in the depression-ridden cotton country of Benton County, Mississippi, she could not have expected a very exciting or eventful future. She lived, however, near the Tennessee state line and only five miles from a bus route taking black students to the Fayette County Training School in Somerville. Since Benton County offered no high school education for blacks, Viola gladly walked the ten miles each

day to attend classes in Tennessee. Here she met and married John Mc-
Ferren. For almost nine years after her graduation from high school,
they quietly farmed the soil of southwestern Tennessee as blacks had
done, first as slaves, and then as tenants, sharecroppers, and small landowners for 130 years. The voter registration campaign in 1959 changed
this traditional existence.

Although blacks owned much of the property and paid considerable
taxes in Fayette County, whites controlled all public institutions and imposed a code of subordinate behavior upon blacks. Registering to vote
violated this code, and Viola McFerren and other participants in the campaign would have to be reminded of their proper "place." Nearly seven
hundred tenant farmers who sought to register were evicted from the
land; but The Original Civic and Welfare League (with Viola and John
in the lead) organized a "tent city," rallying support from local blacks
and from other sympathetic individuals of both races throughout the
nation. White merchants responded by imposing a total economic "lock
out"of goods and services to Fayette blacks; but they held on, driving as
far as Memphis to get milk for their children and gas for their cars. The
test of wills in Fayette County spread to Haywood County and soon received so much national attention that officials from the Justice Department intervened to stop harassment of blacks and end the trade ban.

A new future had begun for Viola McFerren. She and John remained
as leaders of The Original Civic and Welfare League, and the league
continued as the vehicle for racial change in the area. The fear of white
violence did not completely fade for several years, but Viola sustained
her commitment to black equality. She and others tested federal pledges
of support to local blacks by traveling to Washington to obtain aid from
the Federal Housing Administration (FHA) and Small Business Administration (SBA). Later, she played an important role in bringing antipoverty funds to the county and, in turn, served on the national advisory
committee of the U.S. Office of Economic Opportunity (OEO). With
other parents, she filed suit in order to force local compliance with
school desegregation and, as a result, was able to enroll her twins in an
integrated third-grade classroom. By 1969, most of the formal segregation barriers had been knocked down, but Viola McFerren had not

---

Viola McFerren speaking in front of the Fayette County Court House
to a group of black marchers in September 1963. *Courtesy of Viola
McFerren.*

reached her goal. Blacks still suffered from police brutality, unequal protection of the laws, and disrespectful behavior from white merchants. She helped organize a black boycott of local businesses that was expected to continue until corrections and promises of improvement were achieved. After several months, the boycott collapsed short of complete success, but a point had been made: black Tennesseans would not be satisfied until full and meaningful equality had been attained, even in rural West Tennessee.

When the stock market began its rapid descent in 1929, few black Tennesseans were immediately affected. The full impact of the "Great Depression" would reach them soon enough, but in 1929, as members of the most marginal and insecure faction in the economy, they had already begun to feel the tremors of its approaching fury.

Agricultural prices had been in decline for several years, and a sizeable number of black Tennesseans (over 35 percent) still earned their living on the farm. Most black farmers lived in the cotton country of West Tennessee, and the generally declining prices for this once "kingly" product after 1923 had left them, as a group, in a very weak economic position. By 1930 low prices and poor agricultural practices had combined to force more and more black farmers into tenancy (77 percent). For those rural blacks who left the farms and joined the growing numbers in towns and cities, the economic situation in 1929 was not optimistic either. A survey in Nashville that year, for example, showed a decrease of almost 50 percent since 1920 in the types of occupations held by blacks. Skilled opportunities were declining, and approximately 75 percent of all black workers were in the most expendable categories of common and semiskilled laborers. In this, the state's most prosperous black community, average per capita income was only $347.

The most dramatic and ominous omen of future economic troubles came from Memphis. That city's two black banks (the Fraternal and the Solvent) had expanded rapidly during and just after World War I. They invested widely in a variety of housing and business schemes intended to serve and take advantage of the river city's rapidly growing black population. By 1927, however, as with many white-owned banks throughout the state and nation, the black bankers in Memphis saw their empire beginning to crumble under the weight of defaults, poor judgment, and criminal mismanagement. In October the two banks merged in an effort to stave off impending crisis, but Christmas Fund withdrawals caught the institution short of cash reserves and created a disastrous run which forced the doors to be closed. On December 29 it declared bankruptcy.

When the dust from this collapse finally settled, 28,000 depositors (including 7,700 school children) had lost over 90 percent of their savings and more than fifty black-owned businesses had sustained major losses. In a run spawned by the turbulence in Memphis, the Delta Penny Savings Bank of Indianola, Mississippi, failed less than a week after the Fraternal-Solvent closing, and the $100,000 mortgage, loan, and deposit deficits encountered by the National Benefit Life Insurance Company of Washington D.C. started it on a road that led to its demise in 1931.

The unprecedented depression conditions of the early 1930s intensified and expanded the economic troubles of black Tennesseans. Led by cotton, agricultural prices plummeted, and by the end of 1930 over half the rural black population was in need of relief. In the towns blacks, once again, encountered the realities of being the "first fired and last hired." Uncollected accounts and pleas for credit plagued the already precarious position of small black retail and service operations. And the few remaining black financial institutions were sent reeling. In November 1930 the People's Savings Bank and Trust Company of Nashville closed its doors. This bank had pursued a very liberal loan policy throughout its twenty-year existence, purchasing numerous bonds and second mortgages from fraternal and religious institutions as well as making hundreds of loans to workingclass blacks. Defaults had caused concern as early as 1924, but the institution held on until finally "knocked out" by the sweeping punch of the depression. Depositors eventually received 35 percent settlements, but the economic and psychological impact was strongly felt in the capital city.

With the passage of New Deal legislation following Franklin D. Roosevelt's inauguration in 1933, black Tennesseans encountered the most sympathetic and potentially supportive governmental attitudes since Reconstruction. Black farmers joined whites in accepting Agricultural Adjustment Act (AAA) payments for the removal of crop land from cultivation. And unemployed black men turned hopefully to the work relief programs of the Federal Emergency Relief Administration (FERA), Works Progress Administration (WPA), and Civilian Conservation Corps (CCC). Only a small percentage of the available federal funds, however, found their way to blacks in the state. Although they constituted a significant number of the farm operators in Tennessee, most of the $20,000,000 paid to the state's farmers under the AAA was allocated upon the basis of land ownership, and most blacks farmed the white man's land. FERA officials found a great need among black families for relief—tremendous unemployment, an enervating diet dependent upon

fat pork and cornmeal, and an appalling absence of personal property—
but local whites administered the federal funds, and blacks often found
it difficult to get on the relief rolls. WPA daily wages exceeded the fifty to
seventy-five cents paid to day labor by white planters, and this caused
resentment among influential whites. One potential employer complained
to WPA officials in Memphis that "half the Negroes I approached [to
chop cotton] were working for the WPA." Therefore, in spite of their
greater need, blacks made up only a small fraction of the 25,000 persons
employed by the WPA in Tennessee during its six-year existence.

More specific New Deal programs also eased the burden of the Great
Depression for some black Tennesseans. The Farm Security Administration (FSA) made rehabilitation loans to farmers who participated in its
plans for upgrading rural life and improving agricultural practices.
Blacks tended to lag behind in applying for FSA loans in Tennessee, but
they received slightly larger individual grants and had a better rate of re-
payment than whites in the state. The Tennessee Valley Authority (TVA)
operated mostly in East Tennessee during the 1930s, and this area had
only a small black population; but officials promised that hiring would
be non-discriminatory. When black leaders visited the Norris area at the
end of 1933, however, they discovered only two black TVA employees
from the entire twelve-county area. This disclosure encouraged the hiring of a significant number of black laborers, but a NAACP investigation
made the following year revealed that no black workers at the dam or
village sites ranked as high as foreman. Furthermore, their concentra-
tion in the menial jobs gave them "less than 1 percent of the total pay-
roll." TVA also excluded blacks from living in the model village it was
building for the permanent staff at Norris, and by employing blacks
only as menials or in jobs for which they already had trades, the agency
denied them the opportunity to gain new trades and thereby make last-
ing advances as a result of the new economic activity.

New Deal planners gave at least limited attention to the problems of
inadequate housing in the cities. Black Tennesseans had critical needs in

---

(*Above*): Part of the daily lineup outside the state employment service
office in Memphis, June 1938. Farm Security Administration photograph by Dorothea Lange. *Courtesy of the Library of Congress.* (*Below*): Cotton hoers leaving Memphis, bound for the Wilson Plantation
in Arkansas, June 1937. Farm Security Administration photograph by
Dorothea Lange. *Courtesy of the Library of Congress.*

this regard; more than three-fourths of the black residents of Memphis, for example, had lived in obviously substandard housing since the days of the big migration into South Memphis during the Civil War. Although the federal effort throughout the nation was rather half-hearted, "Boss" Crump's influence with Roosevelt was considerable, and he used part of the housing money he obtained to build several segregated housing projects for Memphis blacks. In Nashville, meanwhile, the ninety-three-year-old James C. Napier was appointed to the Nashville Housing Authority in 1938, and the first housing units completed for blacks in the city were named in his honor. The importance of these federally-subsidized housing projects, however, was more symbolic than real; only a few hundred needy blacks benefitted in Tennessee.

In another mostly symbolic gesture, the Reconstruction Finance Corporation (RFC) also came to the aid of black Tennesseans during the depression. The crisis at the People's Bank in Nashville had almost dragged down the only remaining black banking institution in the state. Officials of the unfortunate concern had taken their portfolio to the Citizens Bank (formerly the One-Cent Bank) and asked for either financial support or a merger. Perhaps aware of the earlier difficulties in Memphis, the Citizens Bank refused to extend aid. Shortly after this decision, rumors raced through the black community that it, too, was about to collapse. It survived a run on its reserves at that time by drawing upon the support of the large, white-owned American National Bank, but the hardships of the depression continued to plague the institution. Finally, in 1934, the RFC made a sizeable loan to the Citizens Bank, allowing it (now as the oldest continuously operating black bank in the nation) to avoid bankruptcy.

Even the most liberal Washington planners faced a practical racial decision in the conservative and defensive South. Southern congressional influence had to be considered before challenging any aspect of the caste system. Nevertheless, the dream of equal opportunity and participation in American life flickered cautiously in the minds of black Tennesseans. The federal government had become approachable again, and even life-long Republicans such as Knoxville's Charles Cansler recognized this and joined the growing black political support for Roosevelt and the Democratic party.

(*Above*): Black workers on the Tennessee Valley Authority's Douglas Dam, 1942. *Courtesy of TVA.* (*Below*): Black workers on the Tennessee Valley Authority's Douglas Dam, 1942. *Courtesy of TVA.*

Black Tennesseans, however, also depended upon their own initiative. A black life insurance company had been founded in Memphis in 1923 by Dr. Joseph E. Walker. Known as Universal Life, this firm had barely gotten on its feet when hit with serious losses from the Fraternal-Solvent Bank failure. Even as the company recuperated from the bank jolt, the Great Depression began to take its toll in lapsed policies and uncollected premiums. In the words of company officials, "it was a struggle to keep afloat." Dividends were passed up for several consecutive years, and assets remained almost unchanged from 1930 to 1935. The company's message to its black customers, however, was "employment, jobs, economic progress and home and church financing." Blacks in Tennessee and surrounding states provided enough support for Universal to survive the depression and to grow into a multi-million dollar corporation after World War II.

A few blacks were less patient. Some joined the "radical" and interracial Southern Tenant Farmers' Union in its efforts to organize displaced and exploited farm labor, and perhaps a handful followed former Fisk students, James W. Ford and Merrill Work, into the American Communist party. Most of those who sought rapid improvement, however, chose the more traditional path of migration.

Migration from the farm and rural counties continued. The Memphis black community grew by almost 45 percent during the depression decade, and by 1940, urban residents, for the first time, accounted for more than half (55.5%) of Tennessee's black population. But they brought their poverty-related difficulties with them and found no great improvement until wartime demands created new employment opportunities. Poor housing, high mortality rates, debt, anemia, and general insecurity occurred as readily in Memphis and Jackson as in Glimp and Hickory Withe. Almost half the blacks employed in Tennessee's towns and cities in 1940 performed personal services for whites. Under these circumstances, some migrants could see little difference between ten-cent cotton on the farm and $3.00 per week and an assortment of old clothes and leftover food in town. Many black Tennesseans, therefore, made a second move to a northern city. In the words of black writer Claude Brown, their improvement frequently resembled a climb "from the fire

---

(Left): Black workers on the Tennessee Valley Authority's Douglas Dam, 1942. Courtesy of TVA. (Right): Black workers on the Tennessee Valley Authority's Douglas Dam, 1942. Courtesy of TVA.

into the frying pan"; for housing was no better in Chicago than Chattanooga and the depression-stricken industries of Cleveland, Detroit, and
Pittsburgh offered few promising jobs except as strikebreakers.

Adjustments related to mobility accounted for only part of the social
impact of the depression upon black Tennesseans. Educational opportunities, which had improved dramatically, albeit discriminatorily, for
blacks since 1910, suffered on two fronts. First, the legislature slashed
the state education budget severely in 1933, and political pressure kept
appropriations at a very low level for the next four years. Schools were
closed, teachers went unpaid, and higher education barely stayed alive.
Black institutions, underfinanced anyway, felt the most pain. It took all
the financial maneuvering and skill with the legislature that W.J. Hale
could muster, for example, to keep the doors open at Tennessee A. & I.
For private schools, the situation also became critical. Some black colleges had already closed for lack of students and endowment. Those that
remained open competed with Tennessee A. & I. for recruits among the
900 blacks who graduated from high school annually in the state. But on
a second front, black parents had less and less money to spend on their
children's education. Conversely, they needed more and more family labor in order to meet the basic needs of survival. In short, education had
a low priority during the depression, and black Tennesseans paid a price
in wasted talent and illiteracy.

Black social institutions also suffered. Numerous church buildings
and fraternal lodge halls had to be sold when members failed to meet their
pledges or pay their dues. The Reverend Sutton Griggs, controversial
pastor of the Tabernacle Baptist Church in Memphis, saw his $85,000
multi-facility church foreclosed by Universal Life when his parishioners
failed to make adequate payment on the mortgage. Meanwhile, participation declined among all fraternal groups, and the historian of Prince
Hall Masonry noted that during the 1930s "giant" memberships such as
that found in Tennessee "almost ceased existence." Although some established churches fell on hard times, religion continued to play an important role in black lives. Ministers remained the most prominent
spokesmen in their communities, and urbanization brought a flourish-
ing of storefront Pentecostalism. The Memphis-based Church of God in
Christ, for example, grew from eight local congregations in 1931 to
more than twenty by 1935. Preaching a work ethic that stressed conservative living and avoidance of the dole, this denomination bought the
old Tabernacle Church building and soon had surpassed all but the Baptists among organized religious groups in Memphis.

World War II ended the Great Depression and thus contributed significantly to an improved economic status for black Tennesseans. Men and women found new jobs at the munitions plant near Milan or the super-secret atomic energy project in Oak Ridge; they retrieved old jobs with expansion at the Alcoa plant and at the Chattanooga foundries; and several thousand young men enlisted in the armed forces. Standard of living gains, of course, were moderated by shortages, rationing, and the ever-necessary coupon books. Black Tennesseans did not drive as many cars as whites, but they still worried about buying gasoline and replacing worn-out tires.

They supported the war effort, although rather unenthusiastically at first. Black leaders led war bond drives, and victory gardens once again dotted backyards in black neighborhoods. White selective service boards, however, reflected long-standing fears of military training for blacks and rejected a high percentage of black draftees in Tennessee. But when state NAACP representatives complained to Governor Prentice Cooper about the absence of black representatives on any of the state's draft boards, he dismissed them curtly with the comment that "This is a white man's country. . . . The Negro had nothing to do with the settling of America." Such attitudes were offensive, and so was the naming of Tennessee's primary military induction center after the Confederate General Nathan Bedford Forrest, former slave trader and commanding officer during the infamous Fort Pillow massacre. Most all black Tennesseans who served in the military served in segregated army units, principally in service capacities, and there were several racial "flare-ups" at Tennessee's numerous military installations.

The most sensational and disturbing evidence of racial tension occurred, however, six months after the war ended. A fist fight between two recently-discharged veterans, one black and one white, mushroomed into two days of violence in Columbia, a town forty miles south of Nashville with 11,000 people. Before the episode was completed, a lynching had been narrowly averted, two black men had been killed while in police custody, the entire black business district (known as Mink Slide) had been ransacked and broken up by state troopers, and national publicity had focused upon the small Middle Tennessee town. The key to such conflicts as the one in Columbia was the same as it had been in Knoxville under similar circumstances twenty-seven years earlier. World war had strained traditional caste relationships. Blacks held more important jobs than before the war; they lived in larger and more obvious urban communities; and their military and civilian experiences had given them greater confidence and self-assurance. White superiority was, indeed, threatened by these developments, and abuses of institutional power and personal passion resulted.

Few people recognized it clearly at the time, but the war decade moved black Tennesseans into a period of critical decision. Major developments were taking place in the state, and blacks like Viola McFerren would be greatly affected by the outcome. Agriculture was being revolutionized by mechanization, educational expenditure and programs were expanding rapidly, and politics was starting a slow climb from the dark ages of one-party government and boss domination. If black Tennesseans were left out when the new guidelines to the future were established, any hope for a loosening of the caste system would be lost, and blacks would fall further behind in their pursuit of progress. The cumulative price of discrimination and exclusion was already high. The median income for black families in the state was only slightly over half that for whites, and on the farms, fewer than 5 percent of the tractors in the state belonged to blacks. The median black education level was 6.5 years compared with 8.6 years for whites. And with the decline of Robert Church's power in Memphis during the 1930s, blacks had lost their last significant exercise of political independence.

The racially-based caste system persisted, however, within a changing social and political milieu. First, almost two-thirds of the black population in Tennessee was now urban, and urbanization provided a spatial proximity that encouraged greater collective expression. Second, sacrifices made during another world war against oppression made the indignities of discrimination at home less acceptable. And thirdly, New Deal programs and President Roosevelt's rhetoric invited new appeals to the federal government for protection of civil rights.

The combination of pervasive and chafing oppression and rising black expectations produced several indications that black Tennesseans would not be passive regarding their place in the rapidly changing post-war society. In Memphis several black businessmen, led by Dr. J.E. Walker of Universal Life and bouyed by war-time prosperity and the city's fast-growing black population, founded the Tri-State Bank in 1946. Neither past banking failures nor fears of recurring depression dimmed the determination of these black capitalists to take part in the nation's rapid economic expansion. In Nashville, meanwhile, black leaders formed a citywide political organization in 1947 (known as "The Solid Block") in an effort to mobilize the capital city's ignored and apathetic black vote. The organization soon faded from the scene, but political interest grew, and in 1951 Robert E. Lillard and Z. Alexander Looby (a prominent NAACP lawyer during the Columbia riot) became the first black men elected to the city council in thirty-eight years. Memphis black voters also began to show signs of breaking away from the chains of the Crump machine. Many openly supported Estes Kefauver in 1948 when he successfully challenged Crump's control of the state's Democratic party, and they used this independence locally to win concessions in the appointment of black policemen. And prior to the violence in Columbia, Julius Blair, a black druggist, had been trying to organize a boycott of the local movie theater in that town until he and other blacks were allowed to use the same front entrance as whites.

Most importantly, black Tennesseans began to take aim at perhaps the key to the entire caste system — segregated schools. In 1950, thirty Tennessee counties, all having at least some black scholastic population in the ninth- to twelfth-grade range, offered no public schooling beyond the elementary level. Anderson County and a few others bused black high-school-age children as far as fifty miles to attend a segregated school in a neighboring county, but most did nothing. In a similar manner, except for the education curricula at Tennessee A. & I., the state provided almost no graduate programs for blacks. Therefore, black Tennesseans, building upon precedents established by the NAACP during the 1930s and 1940s, started litigation against the educational abuses in their state. As a result, the courts ordered the University of Tennessee to desegregate several of its graduate schools (most notably its law school) in 1952, and a case asking the desegregation of Clinton High School (Anderson County) began winding its way toward the Supreme Court in 1950.

Before the Clinton case reached its destination, the Supreme Court, on May 17, 1954, handed down the *Brown* v. *Board of Education* decision. By declaring that the doctrine of "separate but equal" had no place in public education and that "separate educational facilities are inherently unequal," this decision paved the way for the abolition of those caste barriers which had formally prevented the fulfillment of the promises of emancipation and reconstruction. But in Tennessee, as elsewhere, black men and women would have to force the issue; they would have to draw upon the tradition of Ed Shaw and Ida Wells. This meant the emergence of new leaders. The old-line leadership of ministers and school principals was either too wedded to accommodation and compromise or too dependent upon white authority for their livelihood. Some of these men threw off their bonds to the past, but the battles of the 1950s and

1960s were most often led by younger, less patient men and women who, once involved, were willing to risk whatever security they might have enjoyed by continuing to conform to the old system. Viola and John Mc-Ferren, for example, had not been community spokesmen nor had they set out to become leaders. Yet, when the issue was joined, they committed themselves totally. For over a year, they had no source of dependable income because neither one had time to devote to a job or the farm. They "survived on whatever turned up."

The civil rights campaign among black Tennesseans moved haltingly during the 1950s. Important efforts pre-dated the *Brown* decision and were not significantly aided by it at first. Court actions, political pressure, and other challenges to the caste system remained local in their impact and, therefore, generated only modest popular involvement or enthusiasm outside the community where black leaders operated. The NAACP was still the most active "organization," and it worked through local chapters. By the end of the decade, however, the contest over school desegregation and the rising national star of Martin Luther King, Jr., had given at least a veneer of common identity to black civil rights workers in the state. King provided a spiritual symbol of purpose, and the school issue gave tangible meaning to the campaign. In reaching this stage, however, several important battles had already been waged in the state, and these gave a necessary legitimacy to the struggle.

The contest over desegregation at Clinton High School was the most dramatic. Clinton was a small mill town located in East Tennessee, fifteen miles from Knoxville and halfway between the model TVA town of Norris and the new atomic energy-based city of Oak Ridge. As was common in this region, its population of less than 4,000 was almost 95 percent white. When District Judge Robert L. Taylor ordered the local high school to admit black students (previously bused to Knoxville) in the fall of 1956, the town authorities offered no resistance, and with an attitude "of resignation" made preparations for orderly compliance. One year earlier Oak Ridge had become the first southern school system to integrate when eighty-five black students enrolled in the junior high and high school programs without incident. At first it appeared that Clinton, likewise, would have few problems. Twelve black students moved quickly past a small group of white protesters on opening day and were received peacefully by the staff and other students. One black girl was even elected vice-president of her home-room class. By the third day of classes, however, rabid segregationist exhorters had descended upon the town, and these "outside agitators" began to play upon the emotional fears and racial prejudice which always lurked near the surface in the South. As the twelve students walked down to the high school from "Foley Hill," the small black section of town, they now faced a gauntlet of men and women with "hate-contorted faces" shouting insults and threatening violence. And, as one of their white teachers noted, "each morning the twelve children marched straight ahead in a body, seemingly unmindful of those who shouted vile names. The boys led the way and the girls followed close behind them."

Agitators came and went, were arrested, and made bail. The National Guard parked its tanks in courthouse square and for ten days in September gave the town an "occupied" appearance. And for four months the black students made their lonely trek down the hill to a chorus of abuse. After Christmas vacation, however, Clinton became quiet and disappeared from the state's newspaper headlines. Only six of the black students withstood the strain and stayed all year, but one young man — the youth who each day led the way to school — graduated with the rest of his senior class in June. Bobby Cain, therefore, became "the first Negro to be graduated from a state-supported [previously] white high school in Tennessee."

What Bobby Cain and his companions did in Clinton was as important as the NAACP-supported desegregation case itself. By braving "the storm of insult and harassment in the pioneer marches across the segregation line in Clinton," these teenagers stimulated a deep sense of pride among blacks throughout the state. Other parents and students at other schools would be called upon to face those same dangers and indignities, and they would know about the students at Clinton. In retrospect, it was anticlimactic when on Sunday morning October 5, 1958, after twenty months of racial calm, three massive explosions blasted Clinton High School to rubble. The battle in Clinton had already been won, and as the lines slowly moved forward in other communities there would be no retreat.

Desegregation in Nashville created less drama and more litigation. Blacks in the capital city filed suit against the Nashville School Board in 1956 and quickly won a favorable verdict. In response, the board announced plans to desegregate the city's first grade classrooms the following fall (1957). This timid effort also contained very liberal provisions for transfer, and when the new term began, no white parents agreed for their children to attend previously black schools and only nineteen black children were enrolled in previously white schools. By focusing upon the first grade and spreading the small number of black students among several schools (six), white authorities had lessened the effect of their action. Black parents hesitated to expose their six-year-old children to almost certain abuse, and it was harder for the racist demagogues to rally their troops against such young children in so many locations. One of the desegregated schools did receive bomb damage, but Nashville police made it clear that unruly demonstrators would be quickly arrested.

Black plaintiffs, meanwhile, let it be known that they were not satisfied with the first year's progress in Nashville or with the school board's plan to advance desegregation on a grade-a-year basis. They took their case to the Federal Court of Appeals and then to the Supreme Court. Yet, in 1959, that court upheld the grade-a-year method—a process requiring twelve years to complete and whose impact was severely curtailed by free transfers. By 1963, only 773 blacks were attending desegregated schools in Nashville. During that year, the Supreme Court answered another black plea by reversing itself and rejecting the Nashville plan as a failure because it "lends itself to the perpetuation of segregation."

While desegregation captured the spotlight in Clinton and Nashville, an even more basic struggle began in the heart of rural West Tennessee. It began in 1959 as a local voter registration drive to generate political participation among the almost 9,000 eligible blacks in Fayette County. The success of this effort and a court ruling in early 1960 outlawing the county's all white primary brought harsh retaliation from the white community. First, a trade ban was imposed against blacks, and then, after the cotton had been picked, wholesale eviction of black tenants and sharecroppers took place. For many years mechanization had undermined the value of black labor in the cotton counties, but in choosing a time of black political activism to make such massive changes, white employers got their message across. But in 1960 and 1961, blacks were not receptive. John and Viola McFerren and others in The Original Fayette County Civic and Welfare League dug in their heels. A black farmer made land available, and the league acquired ten large army surplus tents as temporary housing for the evicted families.

"Tent City" grew almost daily in population, and another was estab-

---

(*Above*): Three new sharecropper families (Goodwin, Williams, and Frazier) arrive in "Tent City" after being forced off the land for registering to vote in Fayette County. *Courtesy of Viola McFerren.* (*Below*): Food and clothing, arriving here by truck, were sent to the residents of "Tent City" from throughout the nation. *Courtesy of Viola McFerren.*

lished in Haywood County. Families set up housekeeping with cardboard carpets, oil drum stoves, and kerosene lamps. They carried water from the farmhouse and used a single outdoor privy. Their plight attracted national attention and civil rights organizations labeled the new community "Freedom Village." At this point the McFerrens virtually gave up their own personal concerns. Along with others they worked nonstop to coordinate efforts in the hardpressed black communities. The trade ban complicated their task, but they eventually convinced Justice Department officials to intervene on their behalf. Injunctions halted the evictions, and federal pressure eased the ban. Antipoverty funds also began to trickle into the county. It had been a contest of wills and survival— and it was not over—but even the state's most oppressed and vulnerable black community had demonstrated to all observers that the days of accommodation and voluntary submission to caste oppression were over. They had taken a common stand, they had obtained governmental encouragement, and they had tasted some success.

In Memphis, young black politicians took the lead. Russell Sugarmon, Jr., Ben Hooks, and A.W. Willis, Jr., had strong personal ambitions and, by 1959, had also grown impatient with Memphis' refusal to make any concessions to desegregation. They set out to apply political pressure upon the city administration by entering candidates in that year's local election. Sugarmon ran for public works commissioner and Hooks sought a juvenile court judgeship. The number of registered black voters in Shelby County had grown from less than 20,000 in 1951 to more than 50,000 in 1959, and the young black politicos hoped to rally this bloc to the polls. If the white vote split as usual, the black candidates stood a good chance of victory. In response to elaborate "Freedom Rallies" and other organized efforts, an unprecedented 63 percent of the registered black voters turned out to vote. All the black candidates went down to defeat, however, when whites responded to their challenge by also voting in bloc and also in unprecedented numbers.

Defeat in 1959 did not discourage the young black politicians. Their clout as spokesmen for an important bloc of voters increased greatly with the return of two-party politics to the state in the mid-1960s. Furthermore, the opportunities to win offices for themselves grew with the

Viola McFerren being interviewed by one of the many news reporters covering the continuing civil rights campaign in Fayette County. *Courtesy of Viola McFerren.*

extensive legislative reapportionment required by the Supreme Court's decision in *Baker* v. *Carr* (1962). Locally and more immediately, one observer took note of the fact that by September 1961 "forty-three Negroes had been appointed to political jobs in Memphis, mostly by men who had run as segregationists before they counted up the precinct returns."

Events in Clinton, Nashville, Fayette County, and Memphis served vitally important preparatory roles, but the concrete changes they wrought were very modest. By 1960 only 169 of Tennessee's 146,700 black school children attended schools even slightly touched by desegregation. And in towns like Oak Ridge, Clinton, and Nashville almost all public accommodations remained just as strictly segregated as they had been in 1954. Rural education for blacks still lagged behind, even within the old separate-but-equal context, and the education debt piled up in the cities as the rural-to-urban migration continued. In 1960, for example, over half of all black men living on farms had less than a fifth-grade education. The median income for black families in Tennessee had actually dropped from 57 percent of the white level in 1950 to 53 percent in 1960. In the state's largest black community in Shelby County, family income was only 44 percent of white family earnings. Housing remained crowded and of poor quality in all black communities. In Knoxville, for example, 50 percent of the houses occupied by blacks received substandard ratings. Black public officeholders were few, and white authorities made only minor concessions in their appointments to government jobs. Tokenism prevailed in fire and police departments, and the duties and authority of black officers were generally restricted to black neighborhoods.

How had the realities of being black and living in Tennessee changed? Historian Hugh Graham has observed that "the biracial system impinged . . . less at the polls and even in the schools than it did in the countless details of everyday life." By 1960 "whites only" signs and "colored day" at the park rubbed sand into the very soul of blacks, particularly younger blacks. At this point a genuine revolution occurred. In black community after black community men and women resolved that to "simply endure" was not enough. *Freedom* could be reached out for and grasped *now*.

The spark came from Greensboro, North Carolina, on February 1, 1960, and it touched off a well-primed direct action movement across Tennessee and the entire South. The sit-in technique enabled blacks to control more of the tempo and focus of change. It helped free them from their susceptibility to the frustrating and momentum-killing delays of litigation and political negotiation. Twelve days after Greensboro, forty students from Fisk and Tennessee A. & I. took seats at the "whites only" lunch counter at Woolworth's in downtown Nashville. Other groups went to Kress's, McClellan's, Grant's, and Walgreen's. On February 22, black high school students took the challenge to the segregated lunch counters in Chattanooga. On March 18 college and high school students launched their attack upon Memphis. And in June, Knoxville College students and staff sat in at several stores in that city's business district.

College and high school-age blacks led the direct attack upon Tennessee's caste system in the 1960s. Black lawyers like Z. Alexander Looby, Russell Sugarmon and A.W. Willis made bail and defended those demonstrators who were arrested, and the NAACP followed up the sit-ins with political negotiations and legal pressure, but the initiative came from the students. Fisk University not only provided much of the leadership in Nashville, but students from that campus soon took the lead throughout the South. Marion Barry, Diane Nash, and John Lewis, for example, were founders of the Student Nonviolent Coordinating Committee (SNCC) and responsible for its controlled, but demanding approach in the early years. (Marion Barry grew up in Memphis and had a reputation as an outspoken undergraduate at LeMoyne College. He was a chemistry graduate student at Fisk in 1960. In January 1979 he became mayor of Washington, D.C.) These students could do things that their parents could not. Most of them did not have jobs to lose or families to support, and they, therefore, enjoyed greater freedom from white institutional control. Their sacrifices were personal sacrifices, and they made them freely, courageously, and repeatedly. The civil rights campaign was no longer an unconnected collection of local efforts. The college students gave a less parochial quality to the specific episodes, and the number and frequency of demonstrations provided a strong sense of common cause and group involvement. Racial self-identity and pride swelled to the surface and turned what had been an historically weak force into a major influence upon black attitudes and subsequent public developments in Tennessee.

By June 1960, lunch counters in seven Tennessee cities had opened to black patrons, and the process of desegregation accelerated. Sit-in organizers in Knoxville took out an advertisement in the Sunday newspaper trying to explain why they were dissatisfied: "We cannot get jobs as city bus drivers, even on routes which carry predominantly Negro passengers. . . . We cannot get service at East Tennessee Baptist Hospital, at Presbyterian Hospital, or at St. Mary's Catholic Hospital. . . . We cannot stay at the leading hotels. . . . We cannot point to a single Negro representative on the City Council, the Board of Education, the Knoxville Housing

Authority, the Library Board, the Knoxville Utilities Board, or the Board of Directors of the City Auditorium. . . . We cannot play golf or bowl in Knoxville. . . . We cannot see a first-run movie." *The Tri-State Defender,* a black newspaper in Memphis, summed up the new attitude with the bold headline, "We Want The Whole Loaf Now!" The Supreme Court cooperated in 1963 by striking down the token school desegregation plans of Memphis, Knoxville, and Davidson County. Then in 1964 Congress settled the public accommodations debate by passing a new Civil Rights Act with ample provisions for enforcement. In that same year A.W. Willis, Jr., won election to the state legislature from Memphis. When he took office in 1965, he became the first black representative to the General Assembly in more than seventy-five years. On the more personal and highly emotional level of interscholastic and intercollegiate athletics, Willie Golden, a black senior, captained his white team mates on the Oak Ridge High School basketball team to the semifinals of the 1966 state tournament. The tournament was won by all-black Pearl High School in Nashville — a team led by Perry Wallace who later that spring signed a grant-in-aid with Vanderbilt University and thus became the first black scholarship athlete to play basketball in the Southeastern Conference.

The formalities and obvious structure of Tennessee's caste society crumbled, but many blacks felt that something was still wrong. They began to concentrate upon the more subtle forms of discrimination found in employment, housing, law enforcement, and the decision making process. These problems did not respond so readily to the direct action approach. Although no less real than segregated schools or lunch counters, they were more complex and harder to confront. Discrimination was easier to see than to "prove," and civil rights workers kept encountering rebuffs like that from the assistant chief of police in Memphis who answered charges of brutality in his department with the comment, we deal "primarily in facts and unfortunately we didn't have too many this morning."

Discrimination in employment took many forms. It could be overtly racial such as TVA's traditional practice of hiring blacks almost exclu-

---

Black college students march to the Capitol to protest the dismissal of fourteen "freedom riders" from Tennessee A & I State University, September 1961. *Photograph by Harold Lowe, Jr. Courtesy of the Nashville Tennessean.*

sively for low level jobs. In 1967, for example, of the 168 black TVA employees in the Knoxville area, not one was employed above grade 8 where the more responsible and better paying management positions began. On the other hand, 119 blacks were employed as either maintenance workers, elevator operators, or clerical helpers. Part of the general problem for black workers was that educational deficiencies blocked their entry into many of the newly-developing skilled jobs in the industrializing parts of the state. But it was more than education because as these opportunities began to open up after World War II, whites had monopolized access to the newest technical training. Even for those with skills and training, however, underemployment was a problem. A job application notice in the *Knoxville News-Sentinel* in October 1967 stated the case: "A 47-year-old [black] man is a college graduate with a major in sociology and a minor in English. Has 18 hours of chemistry and biology, some typing. He's a war veteran, has a good work record, likes detail work and working with people; prefers clerical, administrative, or personnel work. Now works as a porter."

Many black Tennesseans found the fight against these subtle inequalities neither as exciting nor as immediately productive and, therefore, drifted out of the civil rights movement. Meanwhile, those who remained with the struggle or who had found their lives not materially improved by the events of the previous decade became increasingly frustrated. Young black veterans of SNCC demonstrations and voter drives spoke angrily of "black power," and they virtually excluded sympathetic whites from their organizations. Black nationalism replaced integration as the socially acceptable racial strategy on many college campuses. And urban unrest spawned violent riots in the black residential "ghettos" of Memphis, Nashville, and Chattanooga.

Martin Luther King, Jr., was assassinated in Memphis on April 4, 1968. His death disgraced the city of Memphis and the state of Tennessee, but it could as easily have happened in any of a dozen other places

---

(*Above*): Anti-segregation demonstrators march in downtown Nashville in March 1963. Carrying the sign in the foreground is John Lewis, Fisk student and later chairman of the Student Nonviolent Coordinating Committee. Photograph by Frank Empson. *Courtesy of the Nashville Tennessean.* (*Below*): A group of black students who enrolled for the first time in 1965 in Fayette County's previously all white schools. *Courtesy of Viola McFerren.*

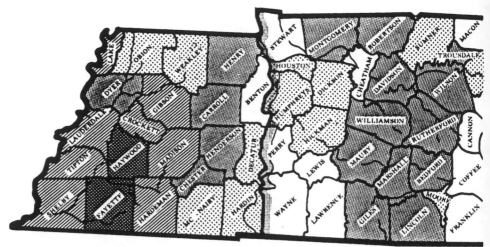

West Tennessee   Middle Tennessee

Distribution of the Black

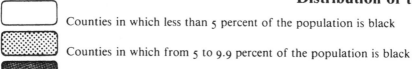

Counties in which less than 5 percent of the population is black

Counties in which from 5 to 9.9 percent of the population is black

Counties in which from 10 to 19.9 percent of the population is black

in America. The tragedy occurred in Memphis, however, because black Tennesseans were struggling in that city to find a way to deal with the continuing problems of poverty and institutional oppression. There had always been one kind of employment "considered most appropriate for blacks: picking up the garbage." In Memphis this task traditionally was performed by recent migrants to the city from the displaced farm labor pool of neighboring Fayette County. The exceedingly poor rural back-ground of these men made them easily exploited by their white super-visors and the city government. During February the American Fed-eration of State, County, and Municipal Employees organized these workers, only to have their demands for recognition rudely rejected by Memphis' hardline Mayor Henry Loeb. The black garbage men went on strike. King was invited in March to address a rally of the strikers and their supporters in the black community. At the time, his leadership and the whole philosophy of nonviolent direct action were being seriously

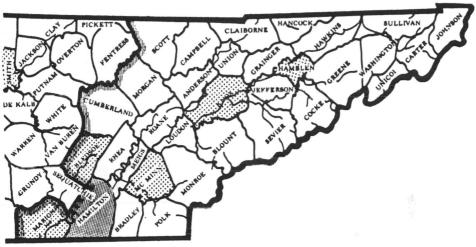

East Tennessee

Population in Tennessee, 1970

 Counties in which from 20 to 49.9 percent of the population is black

Counties in which more than 50 percent of the population is black

attacked by the frustrated younger veterans of the civil rights campaigns. A successful effort in Memphis would help to re-establish his credibility and prevent further fragmentation of black energies. Memphis, therefore, would be an important test to see if King could develop new momentum in dealing with the hard issues left for black Tennesseans in the aftermath of their victories over segregation. Instead, King died and fragmentation and discouragement triumphed — at least temporarily.

If Louis Hughes, Edward Shaw, James C. Napier, and Ida Wells returned to Viola McFerren's Tennessee in 1970, they would see many of their dreams coming true. Hughes would be shocked to see mechanical pickers lumbering through the cotton fields, but he would appreciate the freedom and mobility of former black plantation workers in West Tennessee. Edward Shaw would praise the desegregation decisions and take great satisfaction from the courageous efforts of Bobby Cain in Clinton. Shaw and Napier would set great store by the slow increase in

elected black officeholders (more than thirty in 1970) at all levels of government from schoolboard to legislature and representing all regions
from Knoxville to Somerville. Shaw would have a special personal feeling for Harold Ford's election to Congress from the Eighth District in
1974. Shaw, after all, had been the state's first black congressional candidate 104 years earlier. James C. Napier would be uncomfortable with
the aggressive direct action tactics of black college students in 1970, but
he would be pleased with the attention their efforts had drawn from the
federal government. Most particularly, Napier would commend the aid
given to black businessmen by the Small Business Administration. Ida
Wells would encounter no segregated railroad cars, and even the lunch
counters at the bus station would be integrated. She would applaud the
intervention of federal authorities into the discriminatory practices of
state and local government, and she would praise the aggressive leadership shown by black women like Diane Nash and Viola McFerren.

Why, then, did black Tennesseans begin the 1970s with so little enthusiasm? Integration in the schools provided one answer. The historical
pattern of segregated residential neighborhoods limited the extent of desegregation unless drastic changes were made in the concept of neighborhood schools. Court-ordered busing caused a backlash of white hostility and gave new momentum to the spread of private white schools
and academies. Tennessee politicians had exploited the busing issue during the 1970 elections, and the signals of support from Washington grew
weaker as the Nixon administration's fog of "benign neglect" settled
upon most governmental agencies.

Economic improvements were also highly variable. The determined
stands taken by the black sharecroppers in Fayette County and the garbage men in Memphis had made it clear to white employers that black
workers could no longer be treated as servants. But what about the unemployed and underemployed? Many white collar opportunities had
opened up for blacks, but the hard core of poor and unskilled men and
women made few gains. They remained insecure, marginal workers at
best, and if Louis Hughes passed through South Memphis in 1970 as he
did in 1865, he would still encounter an area of extreme unemployment
(28 percent in 1973), poor housing and sanitation, and high rates of
crime and infant mortality. Memphis, Jackson, and Nashville had begun to benefit from the southward migration of industries and corpo-
rate headquarters, but blacks who sought high paying jobs with these
firms still found themselves at a competitive disadvantage in terms of
education and technical skills. In 1970, 38 percent of all black family in-

comes in the state were below the federally-defined poverty line. For many black Tennesseans, therefore, economic improvements had amounted to little more than increased welfare payments — a kind of benevolent paternalism too often reminiscent of "ration day" on the plantation. And although state and local government had become more responsive in terms of programs and services, the impact of state commitment was limited by a very low tax rate (47th in the nation) and the virtual absence of blacks from decision making positions.

Race relations remained strained, partly by the immediate tensions of the busing issue, but more generally by the fact that events of the past two decades had knocked down a relationship that both blacks and whites at least understood. Now, suspicion and uncertainty prevailed on both sides. Blacks for example, still felt insecure in many of their gains because they came, said Maxine Smith of the Memphis NAACP, not "because white people have recognized their racism, but because black people have continually pushed and pushed." And many black Tennesseans were not even sure they wanted total desegregation of their schools. It would mean losing most of the autonomy and leadership opportunities they exercised in predominantly or all black neighborhood institutions. This racial tension erupted into a fierce riot in Chattanooga in 1971 which left one black resident dead and scores injured before the National Guard finally restored order. Black college campuses continued to experience turmoil. Lane College, for example, had been paralyzed by a student strike for several months in 1969, and before it was settled almost $1 million in buildings and equipment had been destroyed.

The uncertain gains of the 1950s and 1960s pointed out clearly that Tennessee's caste system had been only a sociological manifestation of a deeper psychological force. Black attitudes and freedoms changed markedly from the day of Louis Hughes to that of Viola McFerren, but racial prejudice still posed a *threat* to the dreams of full equality for black Tennesseans.

Appendix

BLACK AND WHITE POPULATIONS OF TENNESSEE
BY GRAND DIVISIONS

	EAST TENNESSEE			MIDDLE TENNESSEE			WEST TENNESSEE		
Census Year	Black		White	Black		White	Black		White
	Slave	Free		Slave	Free		Slave	Free	
1800	5,510	275	67,634	8,074	34	24,075	–	–	–
1810	9,376	510	91,481	35,159	807	124,394	–	–	–
1820	12,421	1,163	124,439	67,445	1,559	221,670	239	9	1,604
1830	17,887	1,944	176,526	97,174	2,199	282,519	26,542	412	76,820
1840	18,714	2,174	203,371	108,433	2,826	307,870	55,912	524	129,386
1850	22,487	2,505	235,405	133,159	3,250	346,770	83,813	667	174,661
1860	27,660	3,284	270,057	146,105	3,228	355,098	101,954	788	201,567
1870		36,769	295,778		157,624	400,712		127,938	239,629
1880		49,623	379,081		180,988	480,882		172,540	278,868
1890		63,725	479,366		176,241	532,343		190,712	324,928
1900		67,487	572,735		183,852	594,340		228,904	373,111
1910		71,833	660,638		169,531	634,141		231,787	416,652
1920		69,877	744,771		147,001	681,381		234,880	459,841
1930		82,715	877,418		135,433	732,963		259,498	528,499
1940		84,175	1,016,924		137,924	818,735		286,637	571,247
1950		90,717	1,198,169		136,038	887,956		303,848	674,132
1960		96,837	1,280,444		145,475	959,663		344,564	737,646
1970		101,242	1,385,523		157,915	1,078,699		372,539	819,210

Selected Readings

The role of blacks in the history of Tennessee has only recently begun to attract the attention it deserves. Historians, students, and other interested readers are discovering that the state's range of geographic, economic, racial, and historical traditions reflects, in many ways, the South in microcosm. The story of black Tennesseans, therefore, is not simple, and it has important implications beyond the borders of the Volunteer State.

Even a brief bibliography should begin with a standard history of Tennessee, and this would be *Tennessee, A Short History* (1969) by Stanley J. Folmsbee, Robert E. Corlew, and Enoch L. Mitchell. In spite of its 600-page length, however, the first edition barely notes the presence of blacks in the state. The revised, second edition, by Corlew, devotes a separate chapter. Paul H. Bergeron's *Paths of the Past: Tennessee, 1770-1970* (1979) gives greater attention to the subject, although the book itself, in the Three Star Books series, is much shorter.

Basic to the understanding of how black men and women have viewed their experiences in Tennessee is the autobiography or firsthand account: Louis Hughes, *Thirty Years a Slave* (rpt. 1969), George L. Knox, *Slave and Freeman,* edited with an Introduction by Willard Gatewood (1979), Charles W. Cansler, *Three Generations* (1939), Ida B. Wells, *Crusade for Justice,* edited by Alfreda Duster (1970), and George W. Lee, *Beale Street: Where the Blues Began* (1934).

For the antebellum period in Tennessee's history only a few published works focus upon or include substantial information regarding black Tennesseans. Edward Michael McCormack's *Slavery on the Tennessee Frontier* (1977) is a readable, but very short and impressionistic account dealing with the late eighteenth century. Chase C. Mooney's *Slavery in Tennessee* (1957) is primarily concerned with the "peculiar" institution rather than the slave. Ira Berlin's *Slaves Without Masters: The Free Negro in the Antebellum South* (1974) is an excellent work with frequent discussions of free blacks in Tennessee. And John Blassingame's *Slave Testimony* (1977) is a collection of slave reminiscences that includes personal material from the lives of several black slaves in Tennessee.

Perhaps no period in Tennessee's history has drawn as much interest as that including the Civil War and Reconstruction. The numerous published works, however, give surprisingly little attention to black Tennesseans in this critical period of their transition from slavery to freedom. Alrutheus Ambush Taylor's *The Negro In Tennessee, 1865-1880* (1941) is basic, and Joseph H. Cartwright's *The Triumph of Jim Crow* (1976) is an excellent study of the direct and indirect importance of black Tennesseans in state politics during the 1880s. But for the important activities of blacks during the Civil War, two unpublished doctoral dissertations must be consulted: John V. Cimprich's "Slavery Amidst Civil War in Tennessee: The Death of an Institution" (Ohio State Univ., 1977) and Bobby Lee Lovett's "The Negro in Tennessee, 1861-1866: A Socio-Military History of the Civil War Era" (Univ. of Arkansas, 1978).

For the period between 1890 and 1950, even fewer published monographs have pursued black themes in Tennessee history. My *Black Tennesseans, 1900–1930* (1977) gives the most extensive coverage, and Roger Hart's *Redeemers, Bourbons and Populists* (1975) and David Tucker's *Lieutenant Lee of Beale Street* (1971) contain important insights into specific areas of black involvement. But for the critical years of the Great Depression and World War II, the published record does not go beyond Tucker's interesting but restricted focus upon George W. Lee in Memphis.

Readers interested in the critical civil rights battles of the 1950s and 1960s in Tennessee can choose from several general sources. Benjamin Muse's *Ten Years of Prelude: The Story of Integration Since the Supreme Court's 1954 Decision* (1964) and Neal R. Peirce, *The Border South States: People, Politics, and Power in the Five States of the Border South* (1975) give considerable attention to events in Tennessee. And Hugh Davis Graham's *Crisis in Print: Desegregation and the Press in Tennessee* (1967) is a valuable analysis of one important aspect of the civil rights story. Other informative works include David Tucker's *Memphis Since Crump: Bossism, Blacks, and Civil Reformers, 1948-1968* (1980) and Merrill Proudfoot's *Diary of a Sit-In* (1962), the latter focusing upon Knoxville.

In selecting works to include in this list, I have confined my choices mainly to published monographs and autobiographies. Frequently, however, some of the most detailed historical information regarding black Tennesseans is found in the issues of such journals as the *Tennessee Historical Quarterly,* the *Journal of Negro History,* the *Journal of Southern History,* the East Tennessee Historical Society's *Publications,* and the West Tennessee Historical Society *Papers.* And yet, after taking all published sources into consideration, many gaps still remain in the record.

Index